At Issue

Should Vaccinations Be Mandatory?

Other Books in the At Issue Series:

At Issue

| Should Vaccinations Be Mandatory?

Roman Espejo, Book Editor

GREENHAVEN PRESS

A part of Gale, Cengage Learning

GALE
CENGAGE Learning·

Farmington Hills, Mich • San Francisco • New York • Waterville, Maine
Meriden, Conn • Mason, Ohio • Chicago

Elizabeth Des Chenes, *Director, Content Strategy*
Cynthia Sanner, *Publisher*
Douglas Dentino, *Manager, New Product*

For more information, contact:
Greenhaven Press
27500 Drake Rd.
Farmington Hills, MI 48331-3535
Or you can visit our Internet site at gale.cengage.com

For product information and technology assistance, contact us at

Gale Customer Support, 1-800-877-4253
For permission to use material from this text or product, submit all requests online at www.cengage.com/permissions

Further permissions questions can be emailed to permissionrequest@cengage.com

Articles in Greenhaven Press anthologies are often edited for length to meet page requirements. In addition, original titles of these works are changed to clearly present the main thesis and to explicitly indicate the author's opinion. Every effort is made to ensure that Greenhaven Press accurately reflects the original intent of the authors. Every effort has been made to trace the owners of copyrighted material.

Cover image copyright © Images.com/Corbis.

LIBRARY OF CONGRESS CATALOGING-IN-PUBLICATION DATA

Should vaccinations be mandatory? / Roman Espejo, book editor.
    pages cm. -- (At issue)
    Summary: "At Issue: Should Vaccinations Be Mandatory?: This title explores the topic in terms of whether the childhood vaccination schedule is safe, whether choice to vaccinate or not should be a right, whether exemptions from vaccinations should be allowed, whether vaccination of healthcare workers should be mandatory, and whether HPV vaccinations should be given to all adolescent girls"-- Provided by publisher.
    Includes bibliographical references and index.
    ISBN 978-0-7377-6862-6 (hardback) -- ISBN 978-0-7377-6863-3 (paperback)
    1. Vaccines--Juvenile literature. 2. Vaccination--Juvenile literature. 3. Medicine, Preventive--Juvenile literature. I. Espejo, Roman, 1977- editor.
    RA638.S55 2014
    614.4'7--dc23
                                               2013041537

Contents

Introduction

All states except for Mississippi and West Virginia allow individuals to apply for religious exemptions to mandatory vaccinations. In 1905, the US Supreme Court affirmed in *Jacobson v. Massachusetts* that states have the authority to administer mandatory vaccinations. The court maintained that "the police power of a State must be held to embrace, at least, such reasonable regulations established directly by legislative enactment as will protect the public health and the public safety." Exemptions are sought for various reasons, such as objecting to the use of aborted fetal tissue as a vaccine ingredient or believing that the immunization for the human papillomavirus (HPV) promotes premarital sex.

Some states just request that the applicant (or the parent or guardian if the applicant is a minor) complete a form indicating that he or she objects to immunization on a religious basis. In other states, obtaining the exemption requires that the applicant practices a religion or belongs to a church that specifically prohibits vaccinations. For example, in its state vaccine requirements, Iowa insists that the applicant demonstrates that "immunization conflicts with a genuine and sincere religious belief and that the belief is in fact religious, and not based merely on philosophical, scientific, moral, personal, or medical opposition to immunizations."[1]

As far as legal cases involving mandatory vaccinations and religious freedom, courts have tended to uphold the state's authority. "Historically, the preservation of the public health has been the primary responsibility of state and local governments, and the authority to enact laws relevant to the protection of the public health derives from the state's general police powers,"[2] observes legislative attorney Kathleen S. Swendiman.

---

1. Iowa Code § 139A.8 Immunization of children.
2. Kathleen S. Swendiman, "Mandatory Vaccinations: Precedent and Current Laws," CRS Report for Congress, February 24, 2011. http://www.fas.org/sgp/crs/misc/RS21414.pdf.

Nonetheless, the constitutionality is not clear cut. According to the College of Physicians of Philadelphia, "courts have often found that requiring parents belong to certain religious groups to qualify for religious exemptions violates the Constitution's Equal Protection clause."[3] Part of the Fourteenth Amendment, it bars a state from denying persons equal protection of the laws in its jurisdiction. "The argument is that the Equal Protection clause should protect all people who claim a religious objection to vaccination, not only those who belong to a certain religion with recognized objections," adds the College of Physicians of Philadelphia.

Proponents contend that religious exemptions to mandatory vaccinations are not only vital to religious liberty but to individual medical choice. "The religious exemption to vaccination is one way you can protect your religious freedom and human right to exercise voluntary, informed consent to medical risk-taking,"[4] argues osteopathic physician Joseph Mercola. "However, also be aware that vaccine exemptions are currently under attack in every state because the wealthy and powerful Pharma/Medical Industry lobby is trying to take them away," he alleges, "especially the religious and philosophical or conscientious belief exemptions." Consequently, Mercola suggests that a person can seek an exemption even if his or her religion or church does not officially object to immunization. "In fact, many organized religions, such as Catholicism, *do* emphasize the 'duty to obey the certain judgment of conscience' and act in ways that do not violate conscience," he explains.

Nonetheless, others warn that religious exemptions place individual and public health at risk. Some health professionals recommend that for communities to maintain herd immunity—in which high immunization rates protect the unimmu-

3. The College of Physicians of Philadelphia, "Vaccination Exemptions," www.historyof
vaccines.org (accessed September 13, 2013). http://www.historyofvaccines.org/content
/articles/vaccination-exemptions.
4. Joseph Mercola, "Using the First Amendment to Opt Out of This Potentially Damag-
ing Procedure," www.mercola.com, December 27, 2011. http://articles.mercola.com
/sites/articles/archive/2011/12/27/legal-vaccine-exemptions.aspx.

nized few and prevent the spread of infectious diseases—the vast majority must be vaccinated. This includes 95 percent of community members for measles and 88 percent for mumps. "Whenever we have pockets of unvaccinated children, we start worrying,"[5] Lorraine Duncan, immunization manager with the Oregon Health Authority, tells *The Wall Street Journal*. She points out that in some areas in Oregon, the religious exemptions rate among schoolchildren is as high as 10 percent and in some areas of the state, 20 percent.

Religious exemptions are one of three types of objections Americans can apply for to forgo vaccines. The other two are medical and personal belief exemptions. "Overall, vaccination rates in the United States remain high. But many experts are wondering what the effect will be on public health of increasing numbers of children being exempted from vaccination," notes the College of Physicians of Philadelphia. In *At Issue: Should Vaccinations Be Mandatory?* the authors offer their views and analyses on this debate as well as the impacts of compulsory immunizations. In particular, this anthology reflects the challenges of balancing public health with civil liberties and the controversies surrounding vaccines.

5. Quoted in Valerie Bauerlein and Betsy McKay, "Where Could the Next Outbreak of Measles Be?" *Wall Street Journal*, March 20, 2012. http://online.wsj.com/article /SB10001424052702303863404577284001227981464.html.

1

Childhood Vaccines Are Important to Public Health

US Department of Health and Human Services

The US Department of Health and Human Services (HHS) is the government's principal agency for serving the health of Americans and providing essential human services.

Producing immunity from 90 percent to 100 percent of the time, childhood vaccines not only have personal benefits, but for entire communities and the future of public health. Improved hygiene and sanitation have helped stop the spread of germs and viruses, but history shows that vaccine-preventable diseases dropped dramatically the years vaccinations were licensed. Vaccines also create herd immunity: In communities where the majority of children are immune, if one child becomes ill, the disease will not spread. However, even though vaccine-preventable diseases are at historic lows in the United States, immunizations are still necessary, as it just takes a few cases of infections to start an outbreak in a population.

The human immune system is designed to protect us from anything that enters our body that doesn't belong there (not including food, of course). Immunologists call these things "non-self."

When a disease organism (that is, a germ—a virus or bacteria) enters the body, the immune system recognizes it as "non-self," and produces proteins called antibodies to get rid

US Department of Health and Human Services, Centers for Disease Control and Prevention, "Part 3: More About Vaccines," *Parent's Guide to Childhood Immunizations*, 2012, pp. 31–37, 39.

of it. These antibodies find and destroy the specific germ that is causing the infection. (For example, antibodies to polio attack polio virus and nothing else.)

But in addition, the immune system *remembers* this germ. Later on, if the person is exposed to the same germ again, antibodies are quickly deployed to eliminate it before it can make the person sick again. This is immunity.

Immunity is why a person who gets an infectious disease doesn't get the same disease again. (There are exceptions: many different viruses can cause the common cold, for example, and flu viruses change from year to year, so existing antibodies might not recognize them.)

This is a very efficient system. There is only one problem with it.

The first time a child is exposed to a disease, his immune system can't create antibodies quickly enough to keep him from getting sick. Eventually they will fight off the infection, and leave the child immune to future infections. But not before child gets sick with the disease.

In other words, the child has to get sick before becoming immune.

Certainly better hygiene and sanitation can help prevent the spread of disease, but the germs that cause disease will still be around, and as long as they are they will continue to make people sick.

Vaccines

This problem is solved by vaccines. Vaccines contain the same germs that cause disease (for example, measles vaccine contains measles virus, and Hib [*Haemophilus influenzae b*] vaccine contains Hib bacteria). But they have been either killed, or weakened to the point that they don't make you sick. Some vaccines contain only a *part* of the disease germ.

When a child is vaccinated, the vaccine stimulates his immune system to produce antibodies, exactly like it would if he were exposed to the disease. The child will develop immunity to that disease, and best of all he doesn't have to get sick first.

This is what makes vaccines such powerful medicine. Unlike most medicines, which treat or cure diseases, vaccines *prevent* them.

How *Well* Do Vaccines Work?

They work really well. No medicine is perfect, of course, but most childhood vaccines produce immunity about 90% to 100% of the time. (What about the small percent of children who don't develop immunity? We'll get to them later.)

But first, what about the argument made by some people that vaccines don't work that well . . . that diseases would be going away on their own because of better hygiene or sanitation, even if there were no vaccines?

That simply isn't true. Certainly better hygiene and sanitation can help prevent the spread of disease, but the germs that cause disease will still be around, and as long as they are they will continue to make people sick.

All vaccines are licensed by the Food and Drug Administration (FDA), and a vaccine must undergo extensive testing to show that it works and that it is safe before the FDA will approve it. Among these tests are *clinical trials*, which compare groups of people who get a vaccine with groups of people who don't. Unless the vaccinated groups are much less likely to get the disease, the vaccine won't be licensed.

If you look at the history of any vaccine-preventable disease, you will virtually always see that the number of cases of disease starts to drop when a vaccine is licensed. . . .

If the drop in disease were due to hygiene and sanitation, you would expect all diseases to start going away at about the same time. But if you were to look at the [history of] polio, for example, you would see the number of cases start to drop around 1955—the year the first polio vaccine was licensed. If you look at the [history of] Hib, the number drops around 1990, for pneumococcal disease around 2000—corresponding to the introduction of vaccines for those diseases.

How Safe Are Vaccines?

This is a question that will naturally concern any new parent. No matter how good vaccines are at preventing disease, no matter how much they have reduced disease over the years, no matter how many lives they have saved, what if they can actually harm my baby?

Vaccine safety is a complex issue. . . . In the meantime, here are some general facts:

Can vaccines harm my child? Any medicine can cause a reaction, even aspirin. Vaccines are no exception.

Will vaccines harm my child? Probably not. Most children won't have any reaction at all to a given vaccine. For those who do, most reactions are very minor . . . a sore leg, a slight rash, or a mild fever that goes away within a day or two.

Some children have moderate reactions like a high fever, chills, or muscle aches.

One of the scariest of these reactions is called a *febrile seizure*. This is a seizure, or convulsion, caused by a high fever. During a febrile seizure a child might shake uncontrollably, become unresponsive, or even lose consciousness. About one child in 25 will have at least one febrile seizure during his childhood, usually between the ages of 6 months and 3 years. They often accompany ear infections or respiratory infections. When a febrile seizure is associated with a vaccine, it is because the vaccine causes a fever, which in turn triggers the seizure. While febrile seizures look serious, fortunately they almost never are. . . .

Rarely, a child may have a truly severe reaction, like encephalopathy (brain infection), or a severe allergic reaction.

These are the scary possibilities that make some parents think that it might actually be better not to vaccinate their children. Would it?

First, severe reactions are extremely rare.

Second, it is sometimes hard to tell whether a reaction was actually caused by a vaccine. Any serious reaction that could be caused by a vaccine could also be caused by something else. There are no serious health problems caused only by vaccines. For something that affects only one child in a hundred thousand or a million, it can be very hard to isolate the cause.

Third, risk doesn't exist in a vacuum. You can't evaluate the risks of vaccination without also considering its benefits.

The risk from a vaccine is the chance it will cause a child serious harm. This risk is extremely small. Even a life-threatening allergic reaction can be brought under control by the trained staff in a doctor's office. . . .

The most obvious benefit of vaccination is, of course, protection from disease. But there is more to it than that. There are really three types of benefits to vaccination—*personal* benefits, *community* benefits, and *future* benefits. It is worth looking at each of these separately:

a) Personal benefits.

Vaccinating your child will protect him from a dozen or so potentially serious diseases.

But how likely is it that your child will actually get one of these diseases? Remember that vaccine-preventable diseases have been declining (thanks to vaccines), and that many of them are now at all-time lows. If the risk of disease is very low, isn't the benefit of vaccination also very low?

Good question. Statistically, the chance of *your* child getting a vaccine-preventable disease may be relatively low. You are making a wager.

If you choose vaccination you are betting that your child could be exposed to disease, so you accept the tiny risk of a serious vaccine reaction to protect him if that happens.

If you choose *not* to vaccinate, you are betting that your child probably *won't* be exposed to disease, or if he is, his illness won't be serious, and you are willing to accept the small risk of serious illness to avoid the small possibility of a vaccine reaction.

Outbreaks of measles, mumps, and whooping cough are occurring around the United States—often among groups of children whose parents have refused to get them vaccinated.

In our opinion, vaccinating is by far the safer bet. Even though diseases have declined, they haven't disappeared. A recent study showed that children who had not gotten DTaP [diphtheria, tetanus, and pertussis] vaccine were *23 times* more likely to get whooping cough than children who had. Thirty-one children died from whooping cough in 2005. That might not be many, but the number wouldn't matter if your child were one of them.

b) Community benefits.

We said that a small percentage of children fail to develop immunity from vaccines. There are also children who cannot get certain vaccines for medical or other reasons, and those who are too young to be vaccinated. These children have no protection if they are exposed to someone who is infected with a communicable disease.

When most children in a community are immune, even if one child gets sick, the disease will probably not spread. That's because it will have nowhere to go—if the sick child comes in contact only with children who are immune, the disease will die out. This is called *herd immunity*.

But when fewer children in a community are immune, it is easier for a disease to spread from person to person and cause an outbreak. [In 2012] Wales was experiencing a "massive" measles outbreak because of parents' failure to vaccinate their children. And outbreaks of measles, mumps, and whooping cough are occurring around the United States—often among groups of children whose parents have refused to get them vaccinated. Recently in California, a boy who contracted measles during a European vacation came back and infected 11 of his unvaccinated classmates.

The point is, we can't stop vaccinating, because even though disease rates are low, they are not zero.

In other words, you are not just protecting your own child by getting her vaccinated, you are protecting other children—adults too.

c) Future benefits.

Rates of vaccine-preventable diseases are very low in the United States. So the risk of an individual child getting, say, a case of measles is very low too. What would happen, then, if we all just stopped vaccinating? We know what would happen because we have seen it in other countries. Diseases that have been declining for years would come back.

The point is, we can't stop vaccinating, because even though disease rates are low, they are not zero. Even a few cases in a vulnerable population could touch off a major outbreak. This is why we still vaccinate against polio, even though we haven't seen it in this country for more than 10 years. One infected traveler from a country where polio *hasn't* been eliminated could set us back 50 years if our own population wasn't protected.

To summarize: When you vaccinate your child, you are not just protecting her. You are also protecting her friends and schoolmates and their families; and you are also protecting her children, her grandchildren, and all future generations.

2

Governments Force Children to Get Vaccinated

Christina England

Based in the United Kingdom, Christina England is an investigative reporter and anti-vaccine advocate. She is a regular contributor to Vactruth.com.

Around the world, governments are pressuring parents to vaccinate their children through elaborate scare tactics. In Australia, it is now mandatory for parents to show documented proof of their children's vaccinations for day care. In the United Kingdom, the media perpetuates a measles epidemic in Wales—year after year—despite the low number of actual infections. And in the United States, efforts to segregate students without chickenpox immunizations took place in Pennsylvania, where they were reportedly refused admittance to prom and graduation ceremonies. While studies show that unvaccinated children are no less protected than vaccinated children, governments—in cooperation with the pharmaceutical industry—continue to devise deceptive ways of increasing childhood vaccinations.

Parents are often misled to believe vaccines are safe and effective.

Countries around the world are coming up with more and more elaborate tricks to pressure parents into fully vaccinating their children. Recently we have seen them telling barefaced lies, denying unvaccinated children access to day care facilities and excluding students from attending their graduation ceremony over a chicken pox scare. To learn more, please continue reading.

Scare Tactics Used in Australia

Over the last few weeks [in 2013], newspapers in Australia have reported that due to the changes being made to the Public Health Act, parents will be forced to produce an up-to-date vaccine certificate, or a conscientious exemption form countersigned by their doctor, if they want to use day care facilities for their children. Any day care facility failing to comply with these new regulations is likely to incur a fine.

According to *The Sydney Morning Herald*, the President of the NSW [New South Wales] branch of the Australian Medical Association, Brian Owler, has declared this "a sensible move." He believes that making parents supply mandatory documentation about their children's vaccination status will boost vaccination rates.

Jillian Skinner, the NSW Health Minister, told reporters:

> "Anyone who has seen a baby with whooping cough or a toddler with measles or has spoken to a parent who has lost a child knows the devastating consequences of failure to vaccinate."

She is absolutely correct, of course; seeing a child with whooping cough is extremely disturbing. However, is vaccination a cast-iron guarantee that your child will be protected? No, it isn't, and I can say this with one hundred percent certainty because my own child contracted whooping cough, despite being fully vaccinated at the time.

Currently, in Australia, vaccination is not mandatory. This is explained very clearly in full in a research paper written by Dr. Viera Scheibner, which we will discuss in just a moment. She says that *"Parents have a constitutional and legal right to opt for natural immunity, which is achieved by contracting the natural infectious diseases of childhood."*

She states that this right is defined in the New Tax System (Family Assistance) Act of 1999, which stipulates that a child is considered immunized if they were administered a vaccine, developed natural immunity by contracting the alleged 'vaccine-preventable' diseases, or if the parents have declared in writing a conscientious objection to the child being vaccinated.

In 2012, Reuters published an article stating that infectious disease specialist David Witt, from the Kaiser Permanente Medical Center in San Rafael, California, reported that his research revealed that the effects of the whooping cough vaccine can wear off over time. He stated, *"We have a real belief that the durability (of the vaccine) is not what was imagined."*

In other words, there has never ever been any real evidence that the vaccine was effective long term. Worrying, isn't it?

The British media had 'accidentally on purpose' reported the SUSPECTED cases of measles, as ACTUAL cases of measles and, in fact, the numbers of confirmed cases were negligible.

Witt's study can be found at *Clinical Infectious Diseases* [journal].

While the Australian government has decided that the best way to boost vaccination uptake is to deny unvaccinated children the right to childcare, the UK [United Kingdom] government has used other dirty tactics to get parents to vaccinate their children.

Scare Tactics Used in the United Kingdom

I am sure that many of you are aware that the UK media recently published a frenzy of reports, highlighting a so-called measles epidemic in Wales. According to newspapers, this epidemic was threatening the lives of two million children residing in the UK.

However, there was never a massive measles epidemic in Wales. The British media had 'accidentally on purpose' reported the SUSPECTED cases of measles, as ACTUAL cases of measles and, in fact, the numbers of confirmed cases were negligible.

Mind you, this latest so-called measles epidemic in Wales is nothing new. Here in the UK, we have heard it all before. In fact, there have been regular so-called outbreaks of measles occurring in Wales for several years.

In 2011, the headlines in Wales stated: *Parents Urged to Get Children Vaccinated as Measles Spreads.*

In 2009, the headlines in Wales stated: *More Parents Choosing MMR* [measles, mumps, rubella] *Jab for Kids During Welsh Measles Outbreak.*

In 2008, headlines in Wales read: *Measles Outbreak in Wales Worsens.*

In 2007, the headlines in Wales stated: *Alert Over Measles as Cases on the Increase.*

Strangely, however, not one of these reports states whether or not the sick children were vaccinated against measles. The reason that this important factor has been left out of reports is because the public is educated to automatically assume that the children most at risk from contracting measles are in fact those who have not yet been vaccinated.

This is untrue, however, because it has been documented for many years that if your child has been vaccinated against measles, there are no guarantees that they are protected.

The Truth About the Measles Vaccine

A paper written by Peter Aaby et al. for *The Journal of Infectious Diseases* in 1986, titled *Vaccinated Children Get Milder Measles Infection: A Community Study from Guinea-Bissau,* states that vaccinated children who contracted measles developed a milder form of the disease. In fact, Aaby's paper states very clearly that vaccinated children are no more protected from the measles than their unvaccinated peers.

In his opening paragraph, Aaby states:

"When vaccinated children develop measles it is usually assumed that seroconversion did not occur because maternal antibodies neutralized the vaccine, because immunoglobulins were administered simultaneously, or because improper handling of the vaccine inactivated it. Numerous cases of 'vaccine failures' have been noted in reports from developing countries. It is often claimed that such failures create a lack of confidence in the immunization program. Some investigators have therefore suggested that the age of the child at vaccination be raised to get a higher rate of seroconversion."

In other words, when a vaccinated child contracts the measles, instead of realizing that the vaccine is ineffective, scientists look for external reasons as to why the vaccination failed. For example, they may look for any environmental factors, which may have contributed.

In this instance, they blame maternal antibodies for seroconversion not occurring and the poor handling of the vaccines. *(Seroconversion is the development of detectable specific antibodies specific to, and in response of a particular antigen, such as a virus or a vaccine.)*

Aaby continued by stating:

"In an urban area of Guinea-Bissau, where measles has been a major source of child mortality, an immunization program was introduced to control the disease. Nonetheless, measles has continued to cause many deaths, and many children are reported to catch measles after vaccination."

Dr. Viera Scheibner's detailed and valuable research supports Aaby's findings. In her paper *A Critique of the 16-Page Australian Pro-Vaccination Booklet Entitled 'The Science of Immunisation: Questions and Answers,'* in the section titled *Effectiveness of Vaccination*, she writes:

"Outbreaks in the fully vaccinated American children continued with increasing frequency and severity. Without disclosing the vaccination status of children in measles epidemics, claiming victory over measles is just empty jabbering.

Moreover, vaccinated children started developing an especially vicious form of atypical measles. [Late physician Vincent] Fulginiti described the occurrence of atypical measles in children given formaldehyde treated, aluminium precipitated measles vaccine, also referred to as 'killed' measles.

He explained the problem as due to the altered immunological host response caused by vaccination."

Up to this point atypical measles had only occurred in children who had received the 'killed measles' vaccine. However, Dr. Scheibner continued by adding:

"Later on, when live attenuated measles vaccine was introduced, the recipients starting developing atypical measles from it, as well."

Dr. Scheibner continues by quoting a study, written by Rath and Schmidt, who studied 386 children who had received three doses of the killed measles vaccine. They discovered that when 125 of these children were later exposed to the measles virus, 54 of them developed measles. The authors concluded:

"It is obvious that three injections of killed vaccine had not protected a large percentage of children against measles when exposed within a period of two and a half years after immunization."

Dr. Scheibner later explains how diseases such as whooping cough and measles can occur in ever-younger children not because the unvaccinated are spreading them, but because babies are born to vaccinated mothers who lack transplacentally transmitted immunity, which normally protects small babies against contracting any infectious disease.

She continues by adding that breastfed babies of vaccinated mothers are three times more likely to catch measles than babies breastfed by naturally immune mothers.

The US government has become so paranoid that unvaccinated children are a danger to the public that they have gone all-out to segregate them.

Various studies support this. A study titled *Waning of Maternal Antibodies Against Measles, Mumps, Rubella, and Varicella in Communities With Contrasting Vaccination Coverage* by Sandra Waaijenborg et al. published in *The Journal of Infectious Diseases* agrees. Waaijenborg's study researches whether using the MMR vaccine "successfully" for twenty years has adversely affected the maternal antibodies passed to infants by their mothers who were vaccinated as children. Her team concluded that:

"Children of mothers vaccinated against measles and possibly rubella have lower concentrations of maternal antibodies and lose protection by maternal antibodies at an earlier age than children of mothers in communities that oppose vaccination. This increases the risk of disease transmission in highly vaccinated populations."

These studies and papers strongly support that vaccinated children still catch the diseases that they are vaccinated against and that vaccines are not only unsafe, but they are also totally ineffective.

Scare Tactics Used in the United States

The US government has become so paranoid that unvaccinated children are a danger to the public that they have gone all-out to segregate them. The most outrageous vaccine segregation that I have ever heard of took place at a school in Norwin, Pennsylvania, recently.

Nine students who had not received the chicken pox vaccination were informed that they would not be allowed to attend their prom unless they either received the chicken pox vaccination or had a blood test proving their immunity.

Despite the fact that study after study confirms that vaccinated children are no more protected than their unvaccinated peers, governments from around the world . . . keep coming up with more elaborate ways to force parents into vaccinating their children.

The panic came after a fellow student caught the disease. However, the students were later informed that they could attend the prom after all because the event didn't fall within the time frame specified to avoid contagion and the school had miscalculated the dates. The health department recommended that students should be excluded eight to 21 days post-exposure to a person with chicken pox.

Pupils were informed that it was unclear whether or not they would be allowed to attend their graduation ceremony, which fell within the period spelled out by the health department.

Sadly, there has been no update on this story, so we do not know if they were allowed to attend their graduation or not.

Denying Parents' and Children's Rights

Despite the fact that study after study confirms that vaccinated children are no more protected than their unvaccinated peers, governments from around the world, hand-in-hand with Big Pharma [pharmaceutical industry] and the medical professionals, keep coming up with more elaborate ways to force parents into vaccinating their children.

I find it very sad that governments are so keen to boost vaccination targets that they are denying parents the ability to earn a livelihood by denying their children's admittance into day care. This seems to me to be over the top and completely unnecessary. How do governments expect parents to be able to support their family if their children are denied access to day care provisions?

Social play is an essential part of a child's development and to deny children the right to play with their peers in a safe play environment purely because they are not vaccinated, in my opinion, amounts to little more than child abuse.

How is the Australian government planning to get around parents' right to opt for natural immunity for their children? Are they planning on changing the law to make vaccination mandatory or will they just make it mandatory for parents who use day care facilities?

Furthermore, to deny students the opportunity of attending their graduation ceremony just because they are not vaccinated with the chicken pox vaccine is totally ridiculous. Graduating from high school is one of the biggest days in a student's life. It is a once in lifetime occurrence. Once it is gone, it is gone.

It is about time that the governments wised up to the fact the unvaccinated children are the most protected children on the planet and that it is the vaccinated that are most at risk of disease and disability. They need to read the work of Dr. Scheibner and the many other researchers who have spent years studying the subject of vaccination and allow children to develop their own natural immunity.

3

The Childhood Vaccine Schedule Is Safe

Institute of Medicine

Institute of Medicine (IOM), the health arm of the National Academy of Sciences, is an independent, nonprofit organization that works outside of government to advise decision makers and the public.

The success of vaccines has spared most Americans from experiencing many serious diseases firsthand. Inoculating children against fourteen pathogens, the recommended childhood vaccine schedule may include up to twenty-four immunizations by the age of two. Therefore, parents have expressed concerns about potential adverse effects, in addition to the schedule being too "crowded" and the risks of immunizations outweighing the benefits. In an evaluation of the literature on the entire childhood vaccine schedule, the evidence does not support links to any serious conditions or reactions, including autoimmune diseases, hypersensitivity, seizures, and child developmental and learning disorders. Still, continuing studies on the safety of the schedule are called for.

Vaccines are among the most effective and safe public health interventions to prevent serious disease and death. Because of the success of vaccines, most Americans have no firsthand experience with such devastating illnesses as polio or diphtheria. Widespread immunizations have resulted in a decline in vaccine-preventable diseases.

Institute of Medicine, "The Childhood Immunization Schedule and Safety: Stakeholder Concerns, Scientific Evidence, and Future Studies (Report Brief)," January 2013. Reprinted with permission from the National Academy of Sciences, Courtesy of the National Academies Press, Washington, DC.

Health care providers who vaccinate young children follow a schedule prepared by the U.S. Advisory Committee on Immunization Practices (ACIP). The current recommended U.S. childhood immunization schedule is timed to protect children from 14 pathogens by inoculating them at the time in their lives when they are most vulnerable to disease. Under the current schedule, which applies to children younger than 6, children may receive as many as 24 immunizations by their second birthday and may receive up to five injections during a single doctor's visit. Technological advances have reduced the number of antigens—that is, inactivated or dead viruses and bacteria, or altered bacterial toxins that cause disease and infection—in vaccines. New vaccines undergo rigorous testing prior to approval by the Food and Drug Administration (FDA). However, like all medicines and medical interventions, vaccines carry some risk.

Some parents' attitudes toward the childhood immunization schedule have shifted, driven largely by concerns about potential side effects from vaccines. In light of this, the Department of Health and Human Services (HHS) asked the Institute of Medicine (IOM) to identify research approaches, methodologies, and study designs that could address questions about the safety of the current childhood immunization schedule. The IOM committee's report, *The Childhood Immunization Schedule and Safety: Stakeholder Concerns, Scientific Evidence, and Future Studies*, summarizes its findings.

The Current Schedule

Newly approved vaccines are tested within the context of the existing ACIP-recommended schedule and are reviewed by clinical researchers who weigh the new vaccine's benefits against its possible risks. Before the ACIP recommends adding a new vaccine to the immunization schedule, it reviews comprehensive data about that vaccine's safety and efficacy in clinical trials, injuries and deaths caused by the disease the vaccine is designed to combat, and the feasibility of adding the new vaccine into the existing schedule, among other factors.

Every year, the Centers for Disease Control and Prevention (CDC) issues guidance on immunization use and schedules for children (birth to age 6), adolescents (ages 7 through 18), and adults, based on these ACIP recommendations.

Stakeholder Concerns

In the course of its work, the IOM committee solicited feedback from a diverse group of stakeholders, including researchers; advocacy groups; federal agencies and advisory committees; the general public, including parents; the health care system and providers; international organizations; the media; nongovernmental organizations; philanthropic organizations; and vaccine-related industries, distributors, and private investors.

More than 90 percent of children entering kindergarten have been immunized with most recommended vaccines in accordance with the ACIP-recommended schedule, according to an analysis of U.S. data. Still, parents, providers, and public health officials agree that there has been insufficient communication between providers and parents about vaccine safety concerns.

Existing mechanisms to detect safety signals—including three major surveillance systems of FDA-approved products maintained by the CDC and a supplemental vaccine safety monitoring initiative by the FDA—provide further confidence that the current childhood immunization schedule is safe.

A number of concerned parents say the schedule is too "crowded" and have requested flexibility, such as delaying one or more immunizations or having fewer shots per visit. Some parents have rejected the vaccines outright, arguing that the potential harm of their child suffering a side effect from the vaccine outweighs the well-documented benefits of immunizations preventing serious disease. Other parents delay or decline immunizations due to worries that family history, the child's premature birth, or an underlying medical condition may make them more vulnerable to complications. Some simply distrust the federal government's decisions about the safety and benefits of childhood immunizations.

While parents generally worry about children's health and well-being, and their concerns about immunization safety can be viewed in that context, delaying or declining vaccination has led to outbreaks of such vaccine-preventable diseases as measles and whooping cough that may jeopardize public health, particularly for people who are under-immunized or who were never immunized. States with policies that make it easy to exempt children from immunizations were associated with a 90 percent higher incidence of whooping cough in 2011.

No Evidence of Safety Concerns

Upon reviewing stakeholder concerns and scientific literature regarding the entire childhood immunization schedule, the IOM committee finds no evidence that the schedule is unsafe. The committee's review did not reveal an evidence base suggesting that the U.S. childhood immunization schedule is linked to autoimmune diseases, asthma, hypersensitivity, seizures, child developmental disorders, learning or developmental disorders, or attention deficit or disruptive disorders.

Existing mechanisms to detect safety signals—including three major surveillance systems of FDA-approved products maintained by the CDC and a supplemental vaccine safety monitoring initiative by the FDA—provide further confidence that the current childhood immunization schedule is safe.

Despite the reassuring available evidence, the committee calls for continued study of the immunization schedule using existing data systems.

Answering research questions of the most importance to stakeholders could be done through a variety of methods. The committee does not endorse conducting a new randomized controlled clinical trial that would compare the health outcomes of unvaccinated children with their fully immunized peers. Although this is the strongest study design type, ethical concerns prohibit this study, as unvaccinated individuals and communities intentionally would be left vulnerable to morbidity and mortality. While stakeholder concerns should be one, but not the only, element that drives continued searches for scientific evidence, the committee writes that these concerns alone, absent epidemiological or biological plausibility of potential safety problems, do not warrant further study.

A new observational study, a complex undertaking that also would require a considerable investment, would be less likely than a randomized controlled clinical trial to conclusively reveal differences in health outcomes between children who are fully immunized and unimmunized children. Fewer than 1 percent of Americans refuse all immunizations. Enrolling sufficient numbers of unvaccinated children and matching them with vaccinated children of the same age, gender, ethnicity, and geographic location—a necessary step to rule out chance findings—would be prohibitively difficult and time-consuming.

The Vaccine Safety Datalink

The IOM committee finds analysis using existing databases to be the most feasible approach to studying the safety of the childhood immunization schedule. It concludes that the Vaccine Safety Datalink (VSD), a collaborative effort between the CDC and nine managed care organizations that monitors potentially rare and serious side effects after vaccines are marketed, is the best available system for studying the U.S. immunization schedule. VSD data represent more than 9 million children and adults—roughly 3 percent of the U.S. population—and include medical details, such as the diagnoses and procedures associated with outpatient, inpatient, and urgent care visits. For this reason, the committee concludes that the VSD is currently the best available system for studying the childhood immunization schedule.

Indeed, rather than exposing children to harm, following the complete childhood immunization schedule is strongly associated with reducing vaccine-preventable diseases.

The committee notes one potential limitation of the VSD: children who are immunized with alternative vaccination schedules may differ in meaningful ways from children who adhere to the schedule, and these differences could make it difficult to tease out health differences that are attributable to the immunization schedule. In order to bridge such data gaps, the VSD system could be modified to enable new analyses of important questions, participants could be asked additional questions, and medical records could be reviewed. The federal government also should continue to build on this component of its robust vaccine safety net by enhancing the quality of VSD's demographic information and including more diversity in its study populations.

Since the late 1970s, IOM committees have conducted more than 60 studies of vaccine safety, attesting to society's sustained interest in safely vaccinating populations from preventable disease. This committee's report is unique in that it is the first to attempt to examine the entire childhood immunization schedule as it exists today.

In this most comprehensive examination of the immunization schedule to date, the IOM committee uncovered no evidence of major safety concerns associated with adherence to the childhood immunization schedule, which should help to reassure a diverse group of stakeholders. Indeed, rather than exposing children to harm, following the complete childhood immunization schedule is strongly associated with reducing vaccine-preventable diseases.

As scientific advances continue and new vaccines are developed, the childhood immunization schedule may grow even more complex. Looking to the future, the IOM supports HHS's efforts to ensure that stakeholders are more fully involved in addressing benefits and concerns regarding the safety of the childhood immunization schedule.

4

The Childhood Vaccine Schedule Is Unsafe

Neil Z. Miller

Neil Z. Miller is director of the ThinkTwice Global Vaccine Institute and author of Vaccine Safety Manual for Concerned Families and Health Practitioners.

Babies are routinely overdosed with multiple rounds of vaccinations; many are injected with more than eight or nine in just one doctor's visit. These vaccines contain a range of dangerous ingredients, including toxins linked to organ damage and neurological disorders. Furthermore, immunizations are not adjusted by infant weight, and babies are not screened for potential adverse reactions beforehand. Numerous vaccines are administered to babies at one time out of convenience, not safety, and such combinations have been shown to cause illnesses in medical experiments. Nonetheless, injuries and deaths caused by simultaneous immunizations go significantly underreported.

Parents need to understand that vaccines are drugs. They contain antigens, preservatives, adjuvants, stabilizers, antibiotics, buffers, diluents, emulsifiers, and inactivating chemicals. They also contain residue from animal and human growth mediums. Here is a partial list of vaccine ingredients, with brief comments.

The Ingredients in Vaccines

Antigens: These are the main components of any vaccine, designed to induce an immune response. They are either weakened germs or fragments of the disease organism: viruses (*polio*), bacteria (*Bordetella pertussis*), and toxoids (*Clostridium tetani*) are examples.

Growth mediums: Viruses require a medium in which to propagate, or reproduce. Common broths include chick embryo fibroblasts; chick kidney cells; mouse brains; African green monkey kidney (Vero) cells; and human diploid cells cultured from aborted human fetuses (MRC-5, RA 27/3, WI-38).

Adjuvants: These are used to enhance immunity. Aluminum salts are the most common and have been linked to neurological disorders.

Preservatives: These are used to stop microbial contamination of vaccines. Thimerosal (mercury) is a recognized developmental toxin and suspected immune, kidney, skin and sense organ toxin. Benzethonium chloride is a suspected endocrine, skin and sense organ toxin. 2-phenoxyethanol is a suspected developmental and reproductive toxin. It is also chemically similar to antifreeze. Phenol is a suspected blood, developmental, liver, kidney, neuro, reproductive, respiratory, skin and sense organ toxin.

Stabilizers: These are used to inhibit chemical reactions and prevent vaccine contents from separating or sticking to the vial. Fetal bovine (calf) serum is a commonly used stabilizer. Monosodium glutamate (MSG) helps the vaccine remain unchanged when exposed to heat, light, acidity, or humidity. Human serum albumin helps stabilize live viruses. Porcine (pig) gelatin, which protects vaccines from freeze-drying or heat, can cause severe allergic reactions.

Antibiotics: These are added to prevent bacterial growth during vaccine production and storage. Neomycin is a developmental toxin and suspected neurotoxin. Streptomycin is a suspected blood, skin and sense organ toxin. Polymyxin B is a suspected liver and kidney toxin.

Additives (Buffers, diluents, emulsifiers, excipients, residuals, solvents, etc.): Some of these, such as sodium chloride, are probably benign. Others, such as egg proteins and yeast can cause severe reactions. Ammonium sulfate is a suspected liver, neuro and respiratory toxin. Glycerin is a suspected blood, liver and neuro toxin. Sodium borate is a suspected blood, endocrine, liver and neuro toxin. Polysorbate 80 (Tween 80) is a suspected skin and sense organ toxin. Hydrochloric acid (added to some vaccines to balance pH) is a suspected liver, immune, locomotor, respiratory, skin and sense organ toxin. Sodium hydroxide is a suspected respiratory, skin and sense organ toxin. Potassium chloride is a suspected blood, liver and respiratory toxin.

The pure and innocent baby is overdosed with 38 vaccine/ drugs by the time he or she is 1½ years old!

Inactivating chemicals: These kill unwanted viruses and bacteria that could contaminate vaccines. Formaldehyde (or formalin) is a known carcinogen and suspected liver, immune, neuro, reproductive, respiratory, skin and sense organ toxin. It is also used in embalming fluids. Glutaraldehyde is a suspected developmental, immune, reproductive, respiratory, skin and sense organ toxin. Polyoxyethylene is a suspected endocrine toxin.

Contaminants: Vaccines may also contain dangerous, unintended substances, such as the carcinogenic monkey virus, SV-40, found in some polio vaccines, and HIV discovered in early hepatitis B vaccines.

The Number of Scheduled Vaccines for Babies

Today, children receive one vaccine at birth, eight vaccines at two months, eight vaccines at four months, nine vaccines at six months, and twelve additional vaccines between 12 and 18 months. The pure and innocent baby is overdosed with 38 vaccine/drugs by the time he or she is 1½ years old!

According to the Centers for Disease Control and Prevention (CDC), babies should get the following vaccine/drug doses before they reach 18 months of age:

- up to 4 doses of the hepatitis B vaccine

- 3 doses of the rotavirus vaccine

- 4 doses of the DTaP shot (for diphtheria, tetanus and pertussis)

- 4 doses of the Hib vaccine (haemophilus influenzae Type B)

- 4 doses of the pneumococcal vaccine (PCV/ Prevnar)

- 3 doses of the polio vaccine

- up to 2 doses of the flu vaccine

- 2 doses of the hepatitis A vaccine

- 1 MMR shot (for measles, mumps and rubella)

- 1 chickenpox vaccine

Babies receive *several* vaccines at each doctor visit. *Many babies receive 8 or more vaccines simultaneously* at 2, 4 and 6 months of age. Imagine ingesting eight or nine drugs all at once. That's what babies are getting. In fact, these babies are not *ingesting* the drugs; instead, the drugs are being *injected* directly into their tiny bloodstreams.

Many babies receive *more* than eight or nine vaccines at once. Since some shot dates are variable (due to "age range" flexibility built into the immunization schedule), *it is permissible for babies to receive a cocktail of up to 13 vaccine/drugs at their 12-month or 15-month doctor visits!*

The vaccines recommended at these ages include DTaP (diphtheria, tetanus, pertussis), hepatitis B, Hib, PCV, polio, flu, MMR (measles, mumps, rubella), chickenpox, and hepatitis A. Up to seven vaccines (for DTaP, hepatitis B, polio, flu, and hepatitis A) can be administered to babies at 18 months.

The general public is essentially unaware of the true number of people—mostly children—who have been permanently damaged or died after receiving several vaccines at the same time.

For Convenience, Not Safety

Several vaccines are administered simultaneously for *convenience*, not safety. Authorities believe that parents are less likely to fully vaccinate their children if they have to make extra trips to the doctor's office. In fact, vaccine manufacturers are not required to test their products in all of the various combinations that they are likely to be used. In addition, vaccines are not adjusted for the weight of the child. For example, a 6-pound newborn receives the same dose of hepatitis B vaccine—with the same amount of aluminum and formaldehyde—as a 12-pound toddler. It is also important to note that babies are not screened prior to vaccination to determine which ones may be more susceptible to an adverse reaction.

Dr. Russell Blaylock has studied toxic synergy. He notes that when two weakly toxic pesticides are used alone, neither causes Parkinson's syndrome in experimental animals. However, when they are combined, they can cause the full-blown disease quite rapidly. He likens this to multiple vaccines administered simultaneously: "Vaccinations, if too numerous and spaced too close together, act like chronic illness."

For similar reasons, Drs. Andrew Wakefield and Stephanie Cave also suggested spacing some vaccines apart (MMR, for example) to lessen the potentially excessive immunological burden on the body. However, it's important to understand that this strategy will not guarantee protection against serious—or even fatal—side effects. Every "body" is different; no two people react the same way. *Single vaccines given separately can, and often do, cause adverse reactions.*

Vaccine Injuries and Deaths Are Underreported

The general public is essentially unaware of the true number of people—mostly children—who have been permanently damaged or died after receiving several vaccines at the same time. *Every year more than 20,000 vaccine adverse reaction reports are filed with the federal government.* These include emergency hospitalizations, irreversible injuries, and deaths. Still, these numbers may be grossly underreported because the FDA [US Food and Drug Administration] estimates that 90 percent of doctors do not report reactions. A confidential study conducted by Connaught Laboratories, a vaccine manufacturer, indicated that "a *fifty-fold* underreporting of adverse events" is likely. Yet, even this figure may be conservative. According to Dr. David Kessler, former director of the FDA, "only about one percent of serious events [adverse drug reactions] are reported." (Multiply reported vaccine reactions by 100 for a more accurate sum.)

The FDA and CDC jointly operate a national database where doctors, nurses and concerned parents can report suspected reactions to vaccines. *These reports—340,000 to date—include children who have been permanently damaged or died after receiving several vaccines simultaneously.*

5

Vaccination Choice Is an Individual Right

Mary Holland

Mary Holland is a research scholar at New York University's School of Law and coeditor of Vaccine Epidemic: How Corporate Greed, Biased Science, and Coercive Government Threaten Our Human Rights, Our Health, and Our Children.

The choice to vaccinate one's self and one's children is a fundamental human right. It is universally recognized that all healthcare interventions must take place under free and informed consent. In practice, mandatory vaccinations protect the majority of the population against diseases while causing injury and death among the genetically vulnerable. This is only justified when individuals, parents, and guardians are provided complete, accurate information of the risks and benefits before electing or refusing to undergo immunizations. Without free and informed consent, mandatory vaccinations violate the rights to liberty and security of person, especially since vaccine manufacturers have little liability for their unsafe products.

Consider the meaning of the phrase *"fundamental human right."* *"Fundamental"* means essential, basic, and inalienable. *"Human"* means what we have simply by virtue of the fact that we are human beings. We are born human; we need not be of a particular age, nationality, gender, or class. A "right" is a claim that we may enforce against governments and other people. Thus we assert that we have inalienable claims we can make within society, simply because we are human beings. The decision of when and whether we vaccinate ourselves and our children is a fundamental human right.

Vaccination choice is a fundamental right because it implicates our most precious rights—to life, liberty, and security of person. Basic laws—such as religious laws, the Universal Declaration of Human Rights, the U.S. Constitution, and international laws that all countries must obey—exist to protect inherent human dignity and the equal and inalienable rights of all members of the human race. Having witnessed the war crimes, genocide, and crimes against humanity committed during World War II, nations of the world explicitly embraced human rights in the United Nations Charter. They recognized that it would be impossible to secure a peaceful, just world without the Universal Declaration of Human Rights that proclaims a "common standard of achievement for all peoples and all nations." In the aftermath of World War II, the world embraced the human rights principles of the Nuremberg Code, a set of ethical principles that forbids experimentation on human subjects without free and informed consent.

Even in circumstances of epidemic disease, compulsory vaccination policies would be suspect without consideration of less invasive alternatives, such as self-quarantine and even coercive quarantine.

Free and Informed Consent Must Be Recognized

Today's human rights laws reject many institutions of the past—slavery, genocide, piracy, torture, inhuman treatment, and systematic discrimination based on race or gender. Some of these laws—such as the prohibition against slavery—have become international norms that apply regardless of whether a particular country has signed a treaty or law to that effect. Today, nations also reject medical experimentation on human subjects without informed consent. Increasingly, nations are recognizing that all healthcare interventions must be based on free and informed consent.

It is an undisputed, scientific fact that vaccines in their current state of development injure and cause death to certain vulnerable people. U.S. law considers vaccines to be "unavoidably unsafe." Vaccination mandates today seek to protect the majority while sacrificing the unknowable, and unknowing, genetically vulnerable few. This utilitarian practice can only be justified if it is based on free and informed consent.

With a complete understanding of the risks and benefits of vaccines, individuals, parents, or guardians may elect to undergo the risks of vaccination to protect against possible disease. They are free to engage in a risk-benefit calculus with their healthcare practitioners and to accept the consequences of their choices. It is unjustifiable, however, for the state to deprive individuals of accurate information and then to coerce them to accept potentially life-threatening medical interventions. Compulsory state vaccination policies violate the rights to liberty and security of person, and when vaccinations result in death, such policies violate the right to life. Even in circumstances of epidemic disease, compulsory vaccination policies would be suspect without consideration of less invasive alternatives, such as self-quarantine and even coercive quarantine.

In the United States, several vulnerable groups—such as children, military personnel, and immigrants—do not have a choice whether to receive vaccinations. Children cannot attend school and adults cannot keep some jobs without fulfilling vaccination mandates. The Vaccine Information Statements that healthcare workers are required by law to give with each federally recommended vaccination are grossly incomplete and often not given at all. Unlike manufacturers of almost all other products, vaccine manufacturers in the United States are legally free from ordinary tort liability for their "unavoidably unsafe" products. The absence of free choice whether or not to use dangerous products, particularly when the manufacturers have exceedingly little liability for them, violates our fundamental rights.

The *Jacobson v. Massachusetts* Decision

States' rights to compel vaccination in this country stem from a 1905 U.S. Supreme Court decision, *Jacobson v. Massachusetts*. In that case, the Supreme Court upheld Massachusetts' right to require adults to be vaccinated during a smallpox epidemic. If the adults failed to comply, the state required them to pay a $5 fine. The Supreme Court found Massachusetts' regulation reasonable for protecting the public's health, but it also pointed out that its decision would not justify "regulations so arbitrary and oppressive" that they would be "cruel and inhuman in the last degree." Based on *Jacobson*, every state now offers at least the formal right to medical exemption from vaccination.

> *Ending compulsory vaccination is its own human rights struggle.*

Overall, *Jacobson* has been interpreted expansively. *Jacobson*, justifying reasonable use of a state's police power, is now the basis for condoning mandates for up to forty-five doses of about one dozen vaccinations for children—in the absence of epidemics, at the cost of public school attendance, based on inadequate and incomplete science, and with significant evidence of undue corporate influence. One may argue today that state vaccination mandates—including compulsory vaccinations for sexually transmitted diseases, such as hepatitis B, and noncontagious diseases, such as tetanus—are oppressive, unreasonable, and disproportionate to the public's health needs. *Jacobson* does not justify today's compulsory vaccination program.

A Thorough Reconsideration Is Overdue

Since *Jacobson* in 1905, the world has embraced human rights in many forms—women's suffrage, the Nuremberg Code, free and informed consent, medical autonomy, the human rights revolution, and public health revolutions in sanitation, hygiene, and antibiotics. A thorough reconsideration of compulsory vaccination mandates is long overdue—based on the language of the *Jacobson* decision, which calls on courts to end vaccination mandates that are oppressive and unreasonable. Even in the context of a military draft, which the *Jacobson* Supreme Court decision refers to by analogy, U.S. citizens have the right to conscientious objection. We must demand the right to philosophical exemption from vaccination mandates in every state as a first step towards truly free and informed vaccination choice.

On many occasions, [civil rights leader] Martin Luther King, Jr. quoted an abolitionist minister from the 1850s, Theodore Parker, saying, "The arc of the moral universe is long, but it bends toward justice." Ending compulsory vaccination is its own human rights struggle. It is time to bend the arc of the moral universe toward the justice of vaccination choice.

6

The Anti-Vaccine Movement Disregards the Great Success of Vaccines

Yoo Jung Kim

At the time of this book's publication, Yoo Jung Kim was an undergraduate researcher at Geisel School of Medicine at Dartmouth and former editor-in-chief of the Dartmouth Undergraduate Journal of Science.

The anti-vaccine movement undermines the scientific consensus that vaccinations are highly effective and beneficial to public health. Present since the very discovery of immunization, opposition today is not based on medical validity, and is comprised of conspiracy theorists, advocates of alternative medicine, and celebrity activists. Their emotionally charged stories and uninformed opinions overshadow the scientific knowledge that supports the efficacy and safety of vaccines. As a result, public confidence in immunizations is eroding and vaccine refusals and exemptions are rising, which creates the risk for dormant diseases to reemerge. The scientific community must counter the anti-vaccine movement and more effectively spread its own message.

In February 2010, *The Lancet*, a preeminent British medical journal, retracted a 1998 article that established a possible link between Measles, Mumps and Rubella (MMR) Vaccines and the development of bowel disease and autism spectrum disorders in young children. An investigative report published by the English newspaper, *The Sunday Times*, revealed that Andrew Wakefield—the article's lead author—manipulated patient data, broke several codes of medical research ethics, and received funding from solicitors seeking evidence to file a litigation against vaccine manufacturers. In 2010, the British General Medical Council ruled that Wakefield held a "fatal conflict" of interest during the course of his research; they found him guilty of multiple counts of serious medical misconduct; and stripped Wakefield of his license to practice medicine. Since then, subsequent papers in respected journals, such as *BMJ*, have debunked the connection between MMR vaccines and autism. Despite Wakefield's fall from grace, however, he has continued to assert the validity of his findings through public lectures and appearances, and his discredited research has further inflamed long-standing oppositions to vaccinations, with possible repercussions for the future of public health.

History of the Vaccine and the Anti-Vaccine Movement

The history of vaccine oppositions spans as far back as vaccination itself. The British Vaccination Act of 1840 was the first case of state-mandated public inoculation, following the experiments of Edward Anthony Jenner. Based on the folk observation that milkmaids were generally spared from smallpox, Jenner, an English general practitioner, postulated milkmaids' direct exposure to cowpox lymph through sores on their hands protected them from the related and more virulent smallpox. He demonstrated that by inserting cowpox lymph into an incision made onto the skin, patients could gain immunity to smallpox. Jenner's idea, novel for its time, immediately met with public criticism. Protesters objected to the idea of infecting seemingly healthy individuals. Members of the clergy claimed that vaccination was ceremoniously unclean, because the body fluid used to confer immunity was derived from animals. Others objected to vaccination because they believed that subsequent government efforts to increase vaccination undermined individuals' rights to control their bodies and those of their children, a tension that escalated with the introduction of mandatory vaccination policies in England.

> *While vaccine technology has evolved tremendously in recent years, the anti-vaccine movement itself has changed little from the anti-vaccine leagues of the nineteenth century.*

Vaccines and the Modern Anti-Vaccine Movement

Vaccination technology has advanced greatly since the crude and direct infections of Jenner's time. Live-attenuated vaccines use lab-weakened microbes that elicit a strong antibody response, which often confers lifelong immunity to the patient. Inactivated vaccines utilize microbes killed by chemicals, heat, or radiation in order to confer immunity, and, although the vaccine is more stable and portable than the live-attenuated counterpart, the effects are generally not as long-lasting. Unlike both live-attenuated and inactivated vaccines, subunit vaccines use only the essential antigens used by the immune system to identify the disease microbe, thereby lowering the chances of adverse side effects.

Current developments in vaccine technology promise increased safety and efficacy. Still in its experimental stages, the DNA vaccine, modeled after the genes of the microbe, would evoke a strong antibody response to the free-floating antigen secreted by cells infected by the microbe and stimulate a strong cellular response against the microbial antigens displayed on infected cell surfaces. The recombinant vaccine, also in its developmental stages, would use an attenuated virus or bacterium to introduce microbial DNA to cells of the body that closely mimics a natural infection and effectively stimulates the immune system.

While vaccine technology has evolved tremendously in recent years, the anti-vaccine movement itself has changed little from the anti-vaccine leagues of the nineteenth century. Its members encompass a vast range of individuals, from conspiracy theorists to educated consumers whose reasons against vaccines stem from a variety of popular reasoning such as "mixture of world views held about the environment, healing, holism . . . and a critical reading of the scientific and alternative literature."

Many vaccine refusers continue to be wary of the growing encroachment of the state over individual health. By the 1980s, all fifty states had passed immunization requirements for public schools, and the vaccination requirements have since grown. Parents today are recommended to give their children thirty shots before the age of six, much more than the dozen or so shots that they received during their own childhood. The increasing requirements have piqued concerns regarding vaccine safety as more parents are taking advantage of states' immunization provisions for vaccination exemptions. As of March 2008, all states permitted medical exemptions from school immunization requirements, 48 states allowed religious exemptions, and 21 states allowed exemptions based on philosophical or personal beliefs.

Other major reasons for vaccine refusal in the United States can be attributed to increasing concern of vaccine safety and a decreasing concern regarding the risk of many vaccine-preventable diseases. Compared with parents of vaccinated children, parents who exempt their children from vaccination generally have a lower opinion of the severity and their children's susceptibility to vaccine-preventable diseases. In a sense, vaccination has become a victim of its own phenomenal success. As more people are vaccinated, the virulence of disease fades away from public memory, and the population's tolerance for side effects—even imagined ones—drops even further.

Frustrated by the lack of answers, concerned parents may mistake correlation as causation and create a state of misinformed fear that could convince other parents to refuse or delay vaccination for their own children.

The activities and theories of the vaccine refusers have been amplified to the general public through the Internet and mass media; a litany of celebrity activists and sensationalist media coverage have overshadowed scientific data. Opinions and speculations have triumphed over scientific consensus that there is no rational reason to fear immunization. Despite the lack of scientific proof, the vaccine refusers are gaining traction. An increasing number of American parents have refused or delayed vaccines for their children, creating a potential health risk for future generations and prompting a re-emergence of long-dormant diseases.

Risk vs. Risk

Concerns regarding vaccines are not unfounded. As a biological product, vaccines do carry real—but very rare—risks, ranging from rashes or tenderness at the site of injection to fever-associated seizures called febrile convulsions and dangerous infections. For instance, oral polio vaccine (OPV), a live-attenuated vaccine, is known to cause roughly one case of the disease per 2.4 million doses—a miniscule risk posed mostly to patients with compromised or underdeveloped immune systems, such as infants, the elderly, chemotherapy patients, and HIV-positive patients.

The risks posed by the extreme rarity of side effects are outweighed by the risk posed by non-vaccination, such as the resurgence of diseases long considered eradicated. For example, between 2001 and 2008, a median of 56 measles cases were reported to CDC annually, yet during the first 19 weeks of 2011, 118 cases of measles were reported—the highest recorded figure since 1996—among which 105 patients were unvaccinated. Children with exemptions from school immunization requirements are at increased risk for contracting measles and pertussis (whooping cough), and may pose a risk to others who are too young to be vaccinated, those who cannot be vaccinated, or those who were vaccinated but are unable to muster a sufficient immunologic response. Because sufficiently high immunization rates must be maintained throughout a given population to prevent future outbreaks, unvaccinated children pose a potential risk to public health.

How to Face the Anti-Vaccination Movement

Despite lack of scientific footing, the anti-vaccine movement is nevertheless fueled by the stories of parents who resolutely believe that immunization has harmed their children. Frustrated by the lack of answers, concerned parents may mistake correlation as causation and create a state of misinformed fear that could convince other parents to refuse or delay vaccination for their own children.

Laws concerning immunization are state-based; as such, the most efficient method to raise vaccination would be for state legislatures to make vaccination exemptions more difficult to obtain—for example, by requiring counseling on the hazards of non-vaccination for parents seeking exemption. Yet, state governments must tread carefully; a heavy-handed approach may threaten individual choice and further inflame the vaccine refusers, whereas a passive approach could potentially undermine public health. As such, in order to maintain high vaccination rates while preserving patient choice, the scientific community and local health providers must place an emphasis on educating the public to enable them to make informed decisions in consideration of the risks posed by vaccination exemption.

Medical providers have an important role in affecting their patient's choices of health consumption. A high proportion of those providing care for children whose parents have refused vaccination and those providing care for appropriately vaccinated children were both found to have favorable opinions of vaccines. However, health care practitioners providing care for unvaccinated children were less likely to have confidence in vaccine safety and less likely to perceive vaccines as benefitting individuals and communities, suggesting a correlation between practitioner and patient opinion.

Secondly, the scientific community must do a better job of disseminating its results to the wider public. Scores of data and professional opinion have gone unheeded, routed by baseless fears and rumors. The sidelining of scientific knowledge by uninformed clamor demonstrates the inability of the scientific community to effectively communicate with the masses, which may set a dangerous precedent for future fears.

According to researchers, the public must be educated in order to regain its confidence in the enormous benefits of vaccinations and to maintain those benefits within the wider society. Furthermore, the scientific community must become more effective in transmitting its message to the wider public, lest its lessons be swept away by the tide of misinformation.

7

Vaccine Exemptions Must Be Protected

Joseph Mercola

Joseph Mercola is a physician and author of numerous books on health and the human diet.

Pro-vaccine groups have shifted the blame on vaccine exemptions for recent infectious disease outbreaks. As a result, citizens are turning against each other, and those with religious, philosophical, or personal objections to vaccinations are fighting for their right to opt out. The majority of infections, however, have occurred among vaccinated people. Naturally acquired immunity is superior to vaccinations, which are failing at higher rates than anticipated. Also, most vaccine recommendations suffer from a conflict of interest; pharmaceutical companies provide indirect benefits to hospitals and their stakeholders in health care. Regardless of vaccination choice, it is a basic right to be fully informed of the risks and benefits and have the option to refuse vaccines.

The featured article in the latest newsletter from Children's Hospital of Philadelphia (CHOP) gets straight to the point with its headline: *Back to School—Is the Child Sitting Next to Yours Immunized?*

The article goes on to berate vaccine exemption options and parents who use personal belief exemptions to opt-out of vaccines for their children. It stops short of ordering parents to march into their children's classrooms and demand to know who's vaccinated and who's not (health privacy laws prevent that anyway).

It peppers you with enough scare tactics—along with links to information on vaccine exemptions and states that allow personal belief exemptions—to leave readers convinced they need to do something to stop vaccine exemptions.

All across the United States, people are fighting for their right to choose not to be injected with vaccines against their will, and this is just the latest tactic in a coordinated effort aimed at eliminating all vaccine exemptions.

The [Bill and Melinda] Gates Foundation is even funding surveillance of anti-vaccine groups. Seth C. Kalichman, professor at the Department of Psychology, University of Connecticut recently received a $100,000 grant to establish an Anti-Vaccine Surveillance and Alert System.

The intention is to "establish an Internet-based global monitoring and rapid alert system for finding, analyzing, and counteracting misinformation communication campaigns regarding vaccines to support global immunization efforts," GreenMedInfo.com reports.

My strong guess is that some of the best sources for truthful information like NVIC.org [web site of the National Vaccine Information Center] and this web site [www.mercola .com] have already been targeted by the Gates Foundation.

Many outbreaks of pertussis (whooping cough), measles, and mumps have occurred primarily in people who were vaccinated, and no one seems to be able to fully explain how that is the fault of those who are unvaccinated.

In light of that, it's not surprising that vaccine groups are trying to turn citizens against each other in an effort to squelch opposition and free will on this matter. According to CHOP:

"... these decisions, often referred to as personal belief exemptions, have been traced to recent cases of pertussis, measles and mumps in several states. Currently, 20 states allow personal belief exemptions.

Many people do not realize that these choices put not only their own children at risk, but also those around them because the more people in a community who are immune to a disease, the lower the chance that the disease will spread throughout the community. This is called herd immunity. So, even those who may not be immune will have a decreased chance of getting the disease."

First of all, there are only 18 states—not 20—that allow personal belief, philosophical or conscientious belief exemptions to vaccination, in addition to 48 states that allow religious belief exemptions.

Unvaccinated Population Falsely Blamed for Ineffective Vaccines

Recent disease outbreaks were traced back to personal belief exemptions . . . Really?

That's just not reality, and if you take the time to look into the truthfulness of that statement, you'll see it simply does not hold up. Many outbreaks of pertussis (whooping cough), measles, and mumps have *occurred primarily in people who were vaccinated*, and no one seems to be able to fully explain how that is the fault of those who are unvaccinated. . . .

If the vaccine theory was correct, these people should have been protected because they were vaccinated. Published studies into the outbreaks have revealed that a lot of the blame should be placed on *ineffective vaccines*—not on the unvaccinated minority.

Consider the following findings about the last two whooping cough (pertussis) outbreaks.

In 2010, the largest outbreak of whooping cough in over 50 years occurred in California. Around that same time, a scare campaign was launched in California by Pharma-funded medical trade associations, state health officials and national media, targeting people opting out of receiving pertussis vaccine, falsely accusing them of causing the outbreak.

However, research published in March of this year [2012] shows that 81 percent of 2010 California whooping cough cases in people under the age of 18 occurred in those who were fully up to date on the whooping cough vaccine. Eleven percent had received at least one shot, but not the entire recommended series, and *only eight percent of those stricken were unvaccinated.*

According to the authors:

> "This first detailed analysis of a recent North American pertussis outbreak found widespread disease among fully vaccinated older children. *Starting approximately three years after prior vaccine dose, attack rates markedly increased, suggesting inadequate protection or durability* from the acellular vaccine." [Emphasis mine]

B. pertussis whooping cough is a cyclical disease with natural increases that tend to occur every 4–5 years, no matter how high the vaccination rate is in a population using DPT [diphtheria, pertussis, tetanus]/DTaP or Tdap vaccines on a widespread basis. Whole cell DPT vaccines used in the US from the 1950's until the late 1990's were estimated to be 63 to 94 percent effective and studies showed that vaccine-acquired immunity fell to about 40 percent after seven years.

In the study cited above, the researchers noted the vaccine's effectiveness was only 41 percent among 2- to 7-year-olds and a dismal 24 percent among those aged 8–12. With this shockingly low rate of DTaP vaccine effectiveness, the questionable solution public health officials have come up with is to declare that everybody has to get *three* primary shots and *three follow-up booster shots* in order to get long-lasting protection—and that's provided the vaccine gives you any protection at all!

The Washington State Secretary of Health also declared a pertussis epidemic on April 3, 2012, in response to a 1,300 percent increase in pertussis cases compared to 2011. Scientists are now considering adding a *seventh* inoculation, in order to boost protection against whooping cough.

According to a recent article and video by KPBS [public broadcasting]:

> "New research confirms the whooping cough vaccine is failing at a higher rate than expected, and scientists are considering adding a seventh dose to the national immunization schedule published by the Centers for Disease Control and Prevention. *Two recent studies have found the majority of people getting sick are up to date with their immunizations.*"

Mumps and Measles Vaccines Are Also Failing

• Mumps: In 2010, more than 1,000 people in New Jersey and New York were also sickened with mumps. In the US, children typically receive their mumps vaccination as part of the Measles, Mumps, and Rubella (MMR) vaccine. The US Centers for Disease Control and Prevention (CDC) advises children to receive their first dose between 12 and 18 months, and their second between the ages of 4 and 6.

This vaccine is supposed to improve immunity to measles, mumps and rubella . . . yet 77 percent of the 1,000+ who came down with mumps were vaccinated. Similarly, in 2006, when mumps infected more than 6,500 people in the United States, cases occurred primarily among college students who had received two doses of MMR vaccine. At that time, just about the only people who were truly immune to mumps were older Americans who had recovered from mumps as children, and therefore had received natural, lifelong immunity.

• Measles—The 1989 measles epidemic in the region of Quebec [Canada] was largely attributed to incomplete vaccination coverage—until a study into the outbreak disclosed that the outbreak occurred in a population that had 99 *percent* vaccination coverage. The researchers concluded that: "*Incomplete vaccination coverage is not a valid explanation for the Quebec City measles outbreak.*"

Conflicts of Interest— Not Science—Influence Most Vaccine Recommendations

The CHOP newsletter is delivered by email periodically to anyone who signs up for it, and almost always contains advice on getting all children vaccinated. The Vaccine Education Center at CHOP says it's funded by endowed chairs and "does not receive support from pharmaceutical companies."

But it neglects to mention that the hospital indirectly benefits from drug company money that helps fund endowed chairs like Merck's Maurice R. Hilleman Professor of Vaccinology, which is currently held by Paul Offit, who not only is very public about his belief that infants could theoretically safely handle 10,000 vaccines all at once; he also openly opposes personal belief vaccine exemptions. Rarely is it mentioned that Offit has a financial stake in the vaccine industry, as he invented one of the vaccines CHOP promotes. He's also served on the scientific advisory board of Merck.

Many still believe vaccines provide identical immunity to that obtained when you are naturally exposed to an infection. This widespread misconception needs to be corrected.

Offit's personal beliefs about forcing people to involuntarily use vaccines, which violates the informed consent ethic in medicine, along with the inaccurate statements he makes about vaccine safety, which are not backed by solid scientific evidence, are echoed throughout CHOP's pro-forced vaccination propaganda. For example, one of their Q&A brochures answers the question: *Can too many vaccines overwhelm an infant's immune system?* with the following statement:

"No. Compared to the immunological challenges that infants handle every day, the challenge from the immunological components in vaccines is minuscule. Babies begin dealing with immunological challenges at birth. The mother's womb is a sterile environment, free from viruses, bacteria, parasites and fungi. But after babies pass through the birth canal and enter the world, they are immediately colonized with trillions of bacteria, which means that they carry the bacteria on their bodies but aren't infected by them. These bacteria live on the skin, nose, throat and intestines. To make sure that colonizing bacteria don't invade the bloodstream and cause harm, babies constantly make antibodies against them.

. . . Given that infants are colonized with trillions of bacteria, that each bacterium contains between 2,000 and 6,000 immunological components and that infants are infected with numerous viruses, the challenge from the 150 immunological components in vaccines is minuscule compared to what infants manage every day."

This is an astounding comparison and shockingly ignorant of foundational physiology.

Not only do these ignorant statements dismiss and disparage the role of beneficial gut bacteria—which we now know are absolutely essential and vital for human health and well-being—and characterize normal gut bacteria as potentially harmful, but there is a false characterization of the immunological challenge posed by multiple vaccines, each of which can contain either live or killed viruses and a number of different adjuvants and chemicals, injected into the tiny body of an infant. CHOP even takes Offit's ridiculous claim that infants can safely handle 10,000 vaccines at one time to brand new heights, stating that:

"The purpose of vaccines is to prompt a child's body to make antibodies, which work by preventing bacteria and viruses from reproducing themselves and causing disease. So, how many different antibodies can babies make?

The best answer to this question came from a Nobel Prize-winning immunologist at the Massachusetts Institute of Technology namcd Susumu Tonegawa, who first figured out how people make antibodies. Tonegawa discovered that antibodies are made by rearranging and recombining many different genes, and found that people can make about 10 billion different antibodies.

Given the number of antibody-producing cells in a child's bloodstream, and the number of immunological components contained in vaccines, it is reasonable to conclude that *babies could effectively make antibodies to about 100,000 vaccines at one time.*" [Emphasis mine]

The Difference Between Natural and Vaccine-Induced Immunity

Many still believe vaccines provide identical immunity to that obtained when you are naturally exposed to an infection. This widespread misconception needs to be corrected.

The presumed result of a vaccination is to help you build immunity to potentially harmful organisms that cause disease. What many fail to appreciate is that your body's immune system is already designed to do this in response to naturally-occurring infectious agents that you are constantly exposed to throughout life. One major difference between vaccine-induced immunity and natural immunity stems from *how* you're exposed to these organisms.

Most organisms that cause infection enter your body through the mucous membranes of your nose, mouth, lungs or your digestive tract.

These mucous membranes have their own immune system, called the secretory IgA immune system. It is a different system from the one activated when a vaccine is injected into your body. Your IgA immune system is your body's first line of defense and its job is to address the infectious microorganism at their entry points, thus reducing or even eliminating the need for activation of your body's entire immune system.

However, when a laboratory altered or created infectious microorganism is injected into your body with a vaccine and, especially when combined with an immune adjuvant, such as aluminum, your IgA immune system is bypassed, stimulating your immune system to mount a very strong inflammatory response.

Since vaccines bypass your natural first-line defense (your IgA immune system), they are clearly inferior to natural immunity and fail to provide the same kind of long lasting protection from future disease as ... what your body would acquire by experiencing and healing from the natural disease.

Vaccines can also trigger such a strong inflammatory response that the inflammation becomes chronic and leads to chronic illness or disability. (People with a personal or family history of severe allergy or autoimmunity should be cautious about vaccination because they already have a genetic predisposition to inflammatory responses that do not resolve and can lead to chronic health problems.)

Injecting these lab-altered microorganisms into your body in an attempt to provoke an atypical, temporary immunity is clearly not the same way your body develops naturally acquired immunity. Your immune system simply was not designed to be injected with lab altered disease-causing organisms in this manner. While I am a great fan and advocate of technology it is very clear to me that this is one reason why vaccines almost always only provide a much more temporary immunity compared to naturally acquired immunity.

Additionally, this plays a large role in why vaccines have the potential to do serious damage to your health.

Since vaccines bypass your natural first-line defense (your IgA immune system), they are clearly inferior to natural immunity and fail to provide the same kind of long lasting protection from future disease as they provide *typically inferior immunity* compared to what your body would acquire by ex periencing and healing from the natural disease. In the case of mumps, for instance, immunity is typically permanent for those who contract the disease during childhood.

What You Need to Know About "Herd Immunity"

The National Institute of Allergy and Infectious Diseases describes vaccine-induced herd immunity, also labeled "community immunity" by public health doctors, as follows:

> "When a critical portion of a community is immunized against a contagious disease, most members of the community are protected against that disease because there is little opportunity for an outbreak. Even those who are not eligible for certain vaccines—such as infants, pregnant women, or immunocompromised individuals—get some protection because the spread of contagious disease is contained. This is known as 'community immunity.'"

There is some serious discrimination against Americans, who want to be free to exercise their human right to informed consent to medical risk-taking when it comes to making voluntary decisions about which vaccines they and their children use.

The problem is that there is in fact such a thing as *natural herd immunity*. But what they've done is they've taken this natural phenomenon and assumed that vaccines will work the same way. However, vaccines do not confer the same kind of immunity as experiencing the natural disease, and the science clearly shows that there's a big difference between naturally acquired herd immunity and vaccine-induced herd immunity. . . .

Why We Must Defend Vaccine Exemptions

All Americans need to know their options for legally opting-out of vaccinations, and you also need to know *why* it's so important to protect this legal option, whether you choose to use every federally recommended vaccine for yourself and your children or not.

No matter what vaccination choices you make for yourself or your family, there is a basic human right to be fully informed about all risks and have the ability to refuse to allow substances you consider to be harmful, toxic or poisonous to be forced upon you.

Unfortunately, the partnership between government health agencies and vaccine manufacturers is getting closer and closer. There is some serious discrimination against Americans, who want to be free to exercise their human right to informed consent to medical risk-taking when it comes to making voluntary decisions about which vaccines they and their children use. We cannot allow that happen!

It's vitally important to know your legal rights and understand your options when it comes to using vaccines and prescription drugs.

8

Widespread Vaccine Exemptions Messing with Herd Immunity

John Timmer

John Timmer is a senior science editor for Ars Technica, *a digital publication focusing on technology.*

Vaccines are one of the most significant and effective public health developments ever. Among children born in one year, scheduled childhood immunizations are estimated to prevent forty-two thousand deaths and twenty million infections. But unfounded fears that vaccines are linked to autism and other serious conditions are influencing more parents to elect vaccine exemptions for their kids, increasing the interaction index, or the frequency a vaccinated student encounters one with an exemption. This adversely affects herd immunity, in which high immunization rates in a given group protect the few individuals for whom vaccines fail or that are unvaccinated due to specific health risks.

*F*alling immunization rates in California are putting children at risk.

Vaccines have been one of the most important public health interventions ever developed. As a new study notes, past analyses have estimated that the childhood immunization schedule prevents 42,000 deaths and 20 million cases of disease—and that's only for the kids born in a single year. The estimated savings is currently at *$14 billion* a year.

But, despite the amazing benefits, immunization rates have been falling, driven by a fear that vaccines cause health problems such as autism. The autism risk has been both thoroughly debunked and the paper that originally suggested it turned out to be the product of an unethical, financially motivated individual. Despite this debunking, surveys show that a quarter of US parents think that vaccines can trigger autism, and rates of vaccination have continued to fall in many states. A new study looks at incoming kindergartners in California, and finds that the lack of vaccination is threatening herd immunity in some schools, and that some measures of risk have doubled in just three years.

California, like other states, has a mandatory immunization schedule, set as a requirement for children entering school. But California is also one of 20 states that allows a personal belief exemption, where parents can file notice that they have a personal issue with vaccines, and get their kids into schools despite a lack of vaccination. The rates of people asking for these exemptions has been slowly climbing, rising from half a percent in 1996 to 1.5 percent in 2007.

Far more students are coming in contact with peers who are unvaccinated—a serious risk, since vaccines are not 100 percent effective.

But the statewide rate only tells part of the story, as the cultural factors that influence vaccine takeup may potentially cluster in certain communities. For example, a measles outbreak occurred in San Diego when an intentionally unvaccinated child picked it up in Europe, and then returned to a school with a high rate of exemptions.

How often is this the case? California health records make it possible to do this sort of analysis, as they include information about the number of exemptions as well as identifying the school the exempted child is attending. The authors of the new analysis combine data on measles vaccinations with some useful statistical tools that were first developed to measure racial segregation within a school system. These include what's called the interaction index, which indicates how often a vaccinated student would encounter someone with an exemption, and the aggregation index, which measures how often exempted students will end up in the same school.

Using data from 2008 to 2010, the authors found some worrying trends. Over just two years, the statewide interaction index increased by 25 percent in this short time. That means far more students are coming in contact with peers who are unvaccinated—a serious risk, since vaccines are not 100 percent effective. Making matters worse, there was also an increase in the clustering of these students. The average exempted student was in a school where 14.7 of 100 students also had exemptions in 2008. By 2010, that number had increased to 15.6.

Herd immunity occurs when a few unvaccinated children are protected by the fact that almost everyone around is vaccinated and therefore cannot infect them. It's important for those for whom vaccines have not worked, those who have immune problems, or those who cannot be vaccinated due to specific health risks. But it requires very high rates of vaccination, typically 80–90 percent. And, in California, it's at risk of breaking down. "The number of kindergartners attending schools in which there were more than 20 exempted kindergartners almost doubled (from 1937 in 2008 to 3675 in 2010)," the authors note.

There were definitely regional issues, as well. In one county in the northern part of the state (Trinity), the average student who started school was in an environment where 13.8 percent of his or her classmates had a vaccination exemption. In Sutter county (just north of Sacramento), the aggregation index was an astonishing 46.3, meaning that every child with an exemption was at a school where nearly half of their classmates would also be exempted.

There are some limits to this study. Some students may be granted an exemption but then ultimately receive all the required vaccinations at a later date, and its authors didn't have access to data like classroom size, which could affect the risk of exposure. But even if these limitations affect the study's precision, the trends it detects are clearly worrisome. About the only bright spot is that the authors note that the tools they have developed can help state officials target educational programs to the communities that need it the most.

9

Mandatory Vaccinations for Health-Care Workers Are Effective

Czarina Biton

Czarina Biton is a senior policy analyst for the Center for Health & Homeland Security at the University of Maryland.

Along with flu prevention, the use of influenza vaccines is associated with reductions in related respiratory illnesses, doctor's visits, hospitalizations and deaths among high-risk groups, and work absenteeism. Yet, among health-care workers (HCWs), who are recommended to get annual flu shots, only half voluntarily receive them. In response, mandatory immunizations for HCWs in health-care systems nationwide are gaining ground, increasing vaccination compliance, preventing flu-related complications and hospitalizations, boosting population immunity, and cutting the costs of flu treatment and sick days. If influenza vaccines are not made mandatory for all HCWs, the well-being and lives of vulnerable groups due to rising infections and complications are at stake.

In the famous words, "an ounce of prevention is worth a pound of cure," our founding father Benjamin Franklin demonstrates his knowledge of principles that would develop the infrastructure of public health preparedness centuries later. During the beginning of the 20th century, infectious diseases such as smallpox, diphtheria, pertussis, tetanus, polio, mumps, measles, rubella, and haemophilus influenzae were common and took a fatal toll on the world's population. The development and administering of vaccines was critical to prevent and control the morbidity and mortality rates of nine preventable diseases and the complications of that time. Immunizations served as a critical form of intervention to effectively combat disease and keep populations healthy in a cost efficient manner.

Influenza or the "flu" has the reputation for being the most deadly disease of human kind, with the first pandemic dating back to 1508. There have been other known pandemics such as the Spanish Flu in 1918 that killed approximately 40 million, with 500 million people ill and most recently in 2009, with the H1N1 strain that killed almost 15,000 people. Because the flu virus spreads through exposure of contaminated air and surfaces, the impact is broad, making it highly contagious. With no known cure, preventing influenza or the "flu" requires the same persistence and science that have been invested in the infectious diseases previously noted. According to the Centers for Disease Control and Prevention (CDC), the use of vaccines to prevent the flu has been associated with reductions in influenza-related respiratory illness and physician visits among all age groups, hospitalization and death among persons at high risk, ear infections among children, and work absenteeism among adults.

The CDC has been recommending that all health care workers get yearly flu shots for 25 years. Despite this recommendation, only half of hospital employees voluntarily get flu shots. The medical and public health community recognize that the hospitals and health care systems need much higher vaccination rates, and have developed and implemented various programs in the country to increase rates. According to the Society for Healthcare Epidemiology of America, voluntary vaccination programs have been in place for decades with little evidence for an overall increase in vaccination rates among health care providers. The momentum of mandatory vaccinations for health care workers (HCWs) is continuing to increase as health care cost rises and our economy recovers. Today, several hospitals and health care systems require health care workers to be immunized against influenza as a condition of employment, with Virginia Mason Medical Center (Seattle, WA) leading the way as the first medical institution to implement such policies.

If you can get close to 100 percent vaccination rates [among healthcare workers], you can cut patient death rates from flu by 40 percent.

History has shown us the health benefits that vaccination offers. However such accomplishments have not gone without controversy. From *Jacobson vs. Massachusetts*, a [1905 US Supreme Court] case that upheld the right of states to enforce vaccinations laws to protect the health of the common welfare, to New York being the first state to establish [in 2009] a directive requiring all HCWs to be immunized against influenza, the emphasis is rightfully on the ethical responsibility and duty to act in the best interest of protecting the general public and to prevent infectious disease outbreaks. This blog article provides you a snapshot of the benefits of immunizing HCWs, the controversy behind mandatory vaccinations and what's at stake if we don't do anything.

The Good—Vaccinating Health Care Workers Benefits Everyone By:

- Increasing compliance and infection control: According to bioethicist Arthur Caplan, PhD, Director of the Center for Bioethics at the University of Pennsylvania in Philadelphia, "If you can get close to 100 percent vaccination rates [among healthcare workers], you can cut patient death rates from flu by 40 percent." In the 2009–2010 flu season, Med-Star Health System, a nine hospital system in Maryland and the District of Columbia, achieved a 98 percent rate compliance after implementing mandatory influenza immunizations to 26,000 employees and affiliated HCWs. Traditional voluntary vaccination programs typically have a 40–50% compliance rate according to the *New York Times*. Doubling the influenza vaccine compliance rates has positive health implications for its patients and workers.

- Preventing complications and hospitalizations: The CDC reports that vaccination is a cost-effective counter-measure to seasonal outbreaks of influenza. A study led by Dr. David K. Shay in February 2008 reported that the flu vaccine was effective in keeping 3 out of 4 people out of the hospital for influenza related complications during the 2005–2006 and 2006–2007 flu seasons.

- Increasing population immunity: According to the Society for Healthcare Epidemiology of America, getting vaccinated against the flu creates a "herd immunity" by protecting those who are vaccinated and those who may be unable to receive vaccines (such as individuals who have allergic reactions to eggs) or those who have compromised immune systems.

- Saving money: Getting sick with the flu not only takes a toll on your body, but also on your pocket. Because you're out sick, there is a direct impact to you due to loss of productivity (not working means no paycheck and fewer things accomplished) and the costs for medical care and medication to alleviate flu symptoms. To look at the cost savings of getting vaccinated, a study published in the *Annals of Internal Medicine* titled "Effectiveness and Cost-Effectiveness of Vaccination Against Pandemic Influenza (H1N1) 2009" estimated the overall cost of vaccinating a city the size of Baltimore-Washington Metropolitan area (around 8.3 million people) is $110 million. According to this study, the short term savings for the city and its residents is equivalent to $686 million in influenza treatment costs. This means that cities and individuals can spend over 6 times less money to prevent the flu by getting vaccinated, versus paying for the treatment, medication and hospital visits to alleviate flu symptoms.

Our country can continue to have a top-notch medical care system if we implement innovative solutions such as mandatory vaccination programs for HCWs.

The Bad—Current Issues Around Mandatory Influenza Vaccinations Include:

- Breach of individual rights: According to the Society for Healthcare Epidemiology of America, a majority of health care workers accept the concept of mandatory influenza vaccination, with one study noting that 70% of respondents believed vaccinations should be mandatory for health care workers who do not have an allergy to the influenza vaccine. Those who oppose this stance believe that such policies are coercive and negatively impact the employee-employer relationship, although there are no available data that support this statement. In fact, healthcare institutions already mandate multiple conditions that reduce the risk of infectious disease transmission [and] require employees to be vaccinated against against varicella, measles, mumps and rubella. Adding influenza to the list of requirements would only continue to maintain the highest level of patient care and service in US medical institutions.

- Misconceptions about the efficacy and safety of vaccine: The misconception about the flu vaccine's effectiveness and safety has also been used as a reason to not get vaccinated leaving HCWs and individuals vulnerable to infection. The reality is, influenza vaccination saves lives, and has a 75% effectiveness in preventing hospitalizations from flu complications. To learn about common misconceptions and the facts, visit the CDC website at: www.cdc.gov/flu/about/qa/misconceptions.htm. In addition, the CDC also recognizes the safety track record of the seasonal influenza vaccine as well as the H1N1 vaccine. According to the CDC, hundreds of millions of Americans have received seasonal flu vaccines and millions of people have also safely received the 2009 H1N1 vaccine. The most common side effects following flu vaccinations are mild, such as soreness, redness, tenderness or swelling where the shot was given. The CDC and the Food and Drug Administration (FDA) monitor for any signs that the vaccine is causing unexpected adverse events and work with state and local health officials to investigate any unusual events.

The Ugly—What Happens If We Do Nothing?

- Increased health complications: According to the CDC, complications of flu can include bacterial pneumonia, ear infections, sinus infections, dehydration, and worsening of chronic medical conditions, such as congestive heart failure, asthma, or diabetes. Influenza risk is not created equal. Unfortunately, specific groups are more vulnerable to the flu, including, children younger than 5, adults 65 years of age and older, pregnant women, and individuals who already have existing medical conditions.

- Increased mortality: The development of vaccines has been recognized as one of the top 10 achievements in public health during the 20th century. Without this innovation, the rate of infection would climb, and with the number of deaths inevitably following that trend. Unfortunately, influenza has no cure and at times, can be fatal, especially to higher risk groups such as the elderly, children under the age of five, pregnant women and individuals with certain medical conditions. Wikipedia notes that the influenza virus is associated with 36,000 deaths and 200,000 hospitalizations each year in the US. From a local perspective, 36,000 deaths amount to filling up all Maryland's acute care beds three times over capacity or having over a third of all students in Baltimore county schools come down with the flu.

Influenza is still one of the top deadliest communicable diseases of our time. Our country can continue to have a top-notch medical care system if we implement innovative solutions such as mandatory vaccination programs for HCWs. Just like the vitamin D that is added into our milk to supplement calcium absorption, the influenza vaccine provides added protection to our immune system to decrease our risk of contracting the highly infectious flu virus. There's a lot at stake if we do nothing, and that is why we should commend the medical and public health institutions for continuing on the path of prevention and addressing the most important aspect of health care: patient safety and positive health outcomes.

10

Mandatory Vaccinations for Health-Care Workers May Not Be Effective

Merrill Goozner

Based in Washington, DC, Merrill Goozner is a senior correspondent for the Fiscal Times *and former director of the Integrity in Science Project at the Center for Science in the Public Interest.*

In the face of worsening flu seasons, mandatory vaccinations for physicians, nurses, and others who have direct contact with patients seems obvious. While drawing objections from labor unions and civil rights advocates, the concerns scientists raise about flu vaccines should prompt health-care administrators to reconsider the requirement. The vaccines are not as effective as government or public health officials claim they are; while figures of 70 percent to 90 percent protection in adults is touted in brochures, the Centers for Disease Control and Prevention (CDC) estimate efficacy at 62 percent. Instead of mandatory vaccinations, voluntary compliance along with other strategies to prevent all infectious diseases should be in place.

The worse-than-normal flu season brings to the fore a troublesome issue for administrators at the nation's hospitals and physician offices: Should physicians, nurses and anyone else with direct exposure to patients be forced to get the annual influenza vaccine?

At first blush, the requirement seems like a no-brainer. If the first precept in medicine is "never do harm to anyone," then facility managers would seem perfectly within their rights to insist that healthcare workers not be allowed to expose vulnerable patients to a potentially deadly virus. A 2011 survey by the Centers for Disease Control and Prevention [CDC] found at least 400 hospitals make the flu vaccine a mandatory condition of continued employment. At least 29 have fired people who refused to comply for other than health or religious reasons. Other hospitals have insisted the unvaccinated wear masks at all times.

The mandatory shot has drawn fire from unions, civil libertarians and some scientists. It is the scientific concerns that ought to give administrators pause, since the evidence backing the efficacy of the flu vaccine is far weaker than either the government or most public health officials like to admit.

How much protection is afforded patients in a doctor's office or hospital if nearly 4 out of every 10 workers, even if inoculated, may be carrying the virus?

Existing Vaccines Far from Adequate

A report issued last fall [in 2012] by the University of Minnesota's Center for Infectious Disease Research & Policy [CIDRAP], whose expert panel included a number of leading public health scientists and drug industry representatives, concluded that existing vaccines are far from adequate in providing "herd immunity" for vulnerable populations. The CIDRAP report also found that calls for universal vaccination—the CDC now recommends annual vaccination for everyone over 6 months of age—"have not always used state-of-the-art scientific data."

The report cited at least 30 examples of government agencies and medical societies exaggerating the benefits of the vaccine. Brochures claim that the vaccine protects against flu in 70% to 90% of adults who receive it; official documents state 50% of deaths among the elderly could be prevented with universal vaccination. (The CDC estimates 89% of the 731,831 people who died from flu between 1976 and 2007 were over 65.)

Yet that's not what the evidence says. Most years, because the precise genetic makeup of the predominant flu strain cannot be known when the vaccine is developed, inoculation provides immunity in slightly more than half the people who receive the shot. This year, because the match was pretty solid, the CDC estimates efficacy at about 62%.

Consistent Protection Remains Elusive

How much protection is afforded patients in a doctor's office or hospital if nearly 4 out of every 10 workers, even if inoculated, may be carrying the virus?

Last week [in January 2013], I spoke with Dr. Michael Osterholm, one of the primary authors of the CIDRAP report. He backs calls for universal vaccination. But he opposes firing people over the issue because it ignores the fact that consistent protection remains elusive for the present generation of vaccines. "If I fix 9 of the 10 screen doors in my submarine, it's still going to sink," he told me.

There may even be risks associated with making flu shots mandatory. Healthcare workers, who are prone to the same misconceptions about the efficacy of the vaccine as the general population, may think they needn't take other precautions to prevent the spread of infection within their facilities if they have had a flu shot. They include proven disease-prevention steps such as frequent handwashing, avoiding direct contact with patients with flu symptoms and limiting visitation at hospitals.

In other words, a reasonable alternative to mandatory vaccination is integrating voluntary campaigns encouraging 100%

compliance into a comprehensive program aimed at eliminating all infectious disease transmission—at least until a better vaccine comes along.

11

Forcing Flu Shots on Health Care Workers: Who Is Next?

Barbara Loe Fisher

Barbara Loe Fisher is president of the National Vaccine Information Center (NVIC) and author of numerous books, including The Consumer's Guide to Childhood Vaccines *and* Vaccines, Autism & Chronic Inflammation: The New Epidemic.

Medical organizations have launched a crusade to coerce every health-care employee to get annual flu shots, setting an alarming precedent for how many vaccinations that Americans will be forced to have to keep their jobs. Established by the US Supreme Court in Jacobson vs. Massachusetts, *vaccine mandates are propped up by the "greater good" principle of utilitarianism, once used to justify experiments on captive human subjects. These violations gave rise to informed consent, protecting people from institutional exploitation and abuses in the name of utilitarianism. Intimidating or firing health-care employees who decline vaccinations is unethical, violating their right to informed consent in medical choices.*

Doctors at Children's Hospital of Philadelphia are ordering all employees to get a flu shot every year or be sent home for two weeks without pay to "think about it." Anyone, who still refuses to get a flu shot after that, is fired.[1]

60 percent of all U.S. health care professionals don't want to get an annual flu shot,[2] which matches the number of Americans, who choose not to get a flu shot, even in pandemic years.[3, 4] Surveys reveal that health care providers know that influenza vaccine can cause nasty, unexpected side effects for some people, like paralysis[5] and convulsions.[6]

Not Just Doctors & Nurses: Everyone

But that has not stopped medical organizations from launching a national crusade to force everyone employed in a "healthcare setting" to get a flu shot every year, whether they have direct contact with patients or not.[7, 8] That's right. Not just doctors and nurses, but every single person who has anything to do with the health care facility, including students, volunteers, and contract workers. An exception could be made if the doctors in charge approve a "medical exemption" to vaccination, which, today, is about as hard to get as a job.

It is not a pretty sight to watch doctors acting more like thugs than healers. When doctors threaten people with financial ruin for refusing to shut up and salute smartly, there is something wrong.

So, even though the 1905 Supreme Court legal opinion was about Americans getting one or two smallpox vaccinations, since then it has been used by doctors to wage an evangelistic crusade . . . by calling on 300 million Americans to be injected with multiple vaccines from day of birth to year of death.

Trust is replaced with fear and anger. People start asking questions. Questions like: Who will be threatened and punished next for refusing a flu shot?

The answer is YOU, me, and every American. We are next in line because when doctors trade in their white coats for military uniforms, going after their own is just the first step on the road to going after the rest of us. If this latest power grab is allowed to set precedent in America, the only question in the future will be: how *many* vaccines will *we* be forced to take or lose our jobs, our health insurance, our right to enter a hospital, or receive medical care, or get on a plane, or check into a hotel if we can't prove we have gotten vaccinated?

1905 U.S. Supreme Court Sets Up Vaccine Pushing & Profit-Making

Vaccine mandates are nothing new in America. After smallpox outbreaks disfigured or killed up to one third of those infected during the 17th and 18th centuries, in 1905 the U.S. Supreme Court gave permission to states to pass laws requiring smallpox vaccination.[9] Since then, that precedent setting Supreme Court case, *Jacobson v. Massachusetts*, has become a kind of holy scripture for public health officials, who have used it to persuade state legislators to pass a whole slew of new vaccine laws barring children from going to school unless they prove they have been injected with dozens of doses of vaccines for infectious diseases that do not come close to being as deadly or contagious as smallpox.[10]

So, even though the 1905 Supreme Court legal opinion was about Americans getting one or two smallpox vaccinations, since then it has been used by doctors to wage an evangelistic crusade to smack down all microorganisms associated with infectious disease by calling on 300 million Americans to be injected with multiple vaccines from day of birth to year of death.[11, 12] This, of course, has created a lucrative boondoggle for pharmaceutical corporations seeking a guaranteed, liability-free market for every new vaccine licensed and sold in America, the third largest nation in the world, which helps these companies finance and develop huge global markets as well.[13, 14] In 2009 alone, multi-national corporations took home profits of $2.8 billion dollars in influenza vaccine sales.[15]

What most people don't realize is that those long dead U.S. Supreme Court judges used a pseudo ethic, utilitarianism, to justify their legal opinion that vaccination should be forced in America. Utilitarianism, which argues that an action is moral if it results in the "greatest good for the greatest number of people," was quite popular at the turn of the 20th century.[16]

The cruel reality of what can happen to individuals when utilitarianism is used to prop up public health policy was brought home in 1927, when U.S. Supreme Court Justice Oliver Wendall Holmes used the *Jacobson vs. Massachusetts* decision to facilitate the forced sterilization of a young woman.[17] At the age of seven months, Carrie Buck was judged to be mentally retarded like her mother. So Holmes gave the green light to the state of Virginia to employ a eugenics solution advocated by medical doctors and scientists and sterilize Carrie for the greater good of society.[18]

Now ... we witness doctors in positions of authority threatening people with loss of employment and financial ruin if they refuse to get injected every year with influenza vaccine, a vaccine that carries two risks: the risk of injury or death and the risk of not working at all.

Justice Holmes said flatly and prophetically, "The principle that sustains compulsory vaccination is broad enough to cover cutting the fallopian tubes."

It is no surprise that Hitler and the Nazis were big fans of Oliver Wendall Holmes.[19] By the way, it turned out that Carrie was not mentally retarded after all.

Crimes Against Humanity & the Informed Consent Ethic

Utilitarianism, like eugenics, was discredited during the Doctor's Trial at Nuremberg after World War II when medical doctors and scientists, who were charged with crimes against humanity, used the utilitarian rationale to justify medical experiments on captive human subjects.[20] The Doctor's Trial in 1946 gave birth to the Nuremberg Code and the ethical principle of informed consent, which has been the guiding principle in the ethical practice of modern medicine since then.[21] Respect for the informed consent principle protects ordinary people from exploitation by wealthy and powerful individuals, corporations and institutions in society, who are in charge of defining "the greater good" and can easily invoke that utilitarian argument to commit civil and human rights abuses.

Take Doctors & Scientists Off the Pedestal

Now, we come full circle to 2010, as we witness doctors in positions of authority threatening people with loss of employment and financial ruin if they refuse to get injected every year with influenza vaccine, a vaccine that carries two risks: the risk of injury or death and the risk of not working at all.

Why are we letting fellow citizens with M.D. or Ph.D. written after their names to tell us what kinds of risks to take with our lives or the lives of our children? Why do we continue to put doctors and scientists on a pedestal in America and fail to put boundaries on the power they too often wield with callous disregard for the informed consent ethic, civil liberties and individual human life?

Influenza Vaccine: You Have the Right to Weigh the Benefits & Risks

Whether or not you are a health care provider, the decision about whether or not to get a flu shot every year is a personal health choice that should be yours to make after you become informed and weigh the benefits and risks. Educated health care professionals and consumers alike are perfectly capable of analyzing the facts about influenza and influenza vaccine, including the fact that:

1. 80 percent of all flu-like illness reported during the "flu season" is NOT caused by influenza but by other viruses and bacteria;[22]

2. Only 5 to 20 percent of Americans get type A or type B influenza in an average year and the majority recover without any complications and are left with immunity to the strains they were infected with, which contributes to natural herd immunity in our population;[23, 24]

3. Like most infectious diseases, influenza can be prevented or reduced in home and health care settings with hand washing, masking and separating sick and healthy persons;[25, 26]

4. Influenza viruses are constantly evolving so, depending upon the year, the flu shot may or may not contain the influenza strains associated with most reported influenza cases;[27]

5. The majority of published influenza studies are so poorly designed, they have not demonstrated that influenza vaccine is effective or safe;[28, 29]

6. Influenza vaccines containing the pandemic H1N1 "swine flu" strain have generated increased reports of paralysis, blood disorders and convulsions;[30, 31]

7. There are no clinical studies to evaluate the long term positive or negative health effects on human populations of being injected with influenza vaccine every year throughout life; and

8. Nobody knows whether mass use of influenza vaccine from the cradle to the grave by all Americans will put pressure on influenza strains to become more virulent like has happened with other microorganisms and universally used vaccines.[32, 33]

Intimidation & Retaliation to Force Vaccination Is Unethical

It is unscientific, irresponsible and a gross waste of health care dollars, especially in these hard economic times, for doctors and scientists in positions of authority to conduct an uncontrolled national medical experiment on the American people by threatening societal sanctions for those who refuse to get a flu shot every year. Firing health care workers, already hit by unemployment, for simply exercising their human right to informed consent to medical risk taking, is unnecessary and unethical.

It is time for Americans to stand up and draw a line in the sand for doctors, who fail to appreciate the difference between offering a medical opinion and giving an order that punishes people for disagreeing with that opinion.

The National Vaccine Information Center [NVIC], which has defended the informed consent ethic in medicine since 1982, joins with other responsible organizations and enlightened individuals, who oppose use of intimidation and retaliation to force all health care professionals to use influenza vaccine.[34, 35] NVIC continues to call for informed consent protections in all vaccine policies and laws in America, including liberal medical, religious and conscientious belief exemptions to vaccination.

Absolute Power Corrupts Absolutely

A British historian, who died three years before the 1905 U.S. Supreme Court justices issued their flawed legal opinion about mandatory vaccination, got it right when he said, "Power corrupts [and] absolute power corrupts absolutely."[36] History has shown that medical doctors and scientists do not know how to wield power without leaving a trail human suffering behind them.

It is time for Americans to stand up and draw a line in the sand for doctors, who fail to appreciate the difference between offering a medical opinion and giving an order that punishes people for disagreeing with that opinion.

References

1. Offit, P. 2010. "Mandating Influenza Vaccine: One Hospital's Experience," *Medscape*.

2. King, WD, Woolhandler, SJ, et al. 2006. "Influenza Vaccination and Health Care Workers in the U.S.," *Journal of General Internal Medicine*.

3. Centers for Disease Control and Prevention. 2008. "State-Specific Influenza Vaccine Coverage Among Adults—US 2006–07 Influenza Season," *MMWR*.

4. Centers for Disease Control and Prevention. 2010. "Interim Results: State-Specific Influenza A(H1N1) 2009 Monovalent Vaccine Coverage—U.S. October 2009–January 2010," *MMWR*.

5. Haber, P., DeStefano, F. et al. 2004. "Guillain-Barre Syndrome Following Influenza Vaccination," *Journal of the American Medical Association*.

6. Corderoy, A. September 19, 2010. "Side Effects Worse than the Disease," *The Sydney Morning Herald* (Australia).

7. Infectious Diseases Society of America and Society for Healthcare Epidemiology of America. Press Release: August 31, 2010. "Nation's Leading Infectious Disease Experts Call for Mandatory Flu Vaccine for All Healthcare Personnel: Vaccines Should be Required for Continued Employment for Healthcare Personnel, Epidemiologists and Infectious Disease Physicians Say."

8. Neale, T. September 8, 2010. "Flu Vaccine a Must for All Healthcare Workers, AAP says," *Medpage Today.*

9. *Jacobson v. Massachusetts*, 197 U.S. 11 (1905), LSU Law Center.

10. CNN. November 15, 2007. "Vaccinations or Jail: County's Threat to Parents."

11. Centers for Disease Control. 2010 Child & Adolescent Immunization Schedules.

12. Centers for Disease Control. Adult Immunization Schedule—2010.

13. *HealthCare Finance News.* 2010. "Global Vaccine Market Now Exceeds $20B."

14. Glorikan, H. 2009. "Influenza Scare Not the Only Vaccine Driver," *Genetic Engineering & Biotechnology News.*

15. Kresse, H., Rovini, H. 2009. "Influenza Vaccine Market Dynamics," *Nature Reviews.*

16. Mautner, T., ed. 2005. "Jeremy Bentham (1748–1832)," *The Penguin Dictionary of Philosophy*, and "Utilitarianism," *The Penguin Dictionary of Philosophy.*

17. "Supreme Court Upholds Sterilization of the Mentally Retarded—*Buck v. Bell*," 274 U.S. 200, 475 Ct. 584, 71L, Ed. 1000 (1927), LSU Law Center.

18. *Encyclopedia of Virginia, Buck v. Bell* (1927).

19. Black, E. November 24, 2003. "The Horrifying American Roots of Nazi Eugenics," *History News Network* (George Mason University).

20. Seidelman, WE. 1996. "Nuremberg Lamentation: For the Forgotten Victims of Medical Science," *British Medical Journal.*

21. Katz, J. "The Consent Principle of the Nuremberg Code: It's Significance Then and Now," *The Nazi Doctors and the Nuremberg Code*. New York: Oxford University Press, 1992, pp. 227–239.

22. FDA, February 20, 2003. "Vaccines & Related Biological Products Advisory Committee" Meeting Transcript."

23. Centers for Disease Control. Seasonal Influenza.

24. Simonsen, L., Clarke, MJ, et al. 1998. "Pandemic versus Epidemic Influenza Mortality: A Pattern of Changing Age Distribution," *Journal of Infectious Diseases.*

25. Enstone, J. 2010. "Influenza Transmission and Related Infection Control Issues," *Introduction to Pandemic Influenza*, pp. 57–72. CABI.

26. Aledort, TE, Lurie, N., et al. 2007. "Non-pharmaceutical Public Health Interventions for Pandemic Influenza: An Evaluation of the Evidence Base," *BMC Public Health.*

27. Fisher, BL. 2004. "Flu Vaccine: Missing the Mark," *The Vaccine Reaction* (National Vaccine Information Center).

28. Jefferson, T. 2006. "Influenza Vaccination: Policy versus Evidence," *British Medical Journal.*

29. Jefferson, T., Debalini, MG, et al. 2009. "Relation of Study Quality, Concordance, Take Home Message, Funding, and Impact in Studies of Influenza Vaccines; Systematic Review," *British Medical Journal.*

30. National Vaccine Information Center. 2010. Press Release: "NVIC Calls for Expanded Monitoring of Pandemic H1N1 Vaccine Reactions."

31. Collignon, P., Doshi, P., and Jefferson. T. 2010. "Adverse Events Following Influenza Vaccination in Australia—Should We Be Surprised?" *British Medical Journal.*

32. Associated Press. September 17, 2007. "Shot May Be Inadvertently Boosting Superbugs," MSNBC.

33. Fisher, BL. July 8, 2010. "Whooping Cough Outbreaks and Vaccine Failures," National Vaccine Information Center.

34. ACLU. 2009. "NYCLU Urges Public Education and Voluntary Vaccine for H1N1 Flu," Warns Vaccine Mandate Violates Privacy Rights, testimony by Donna Lieberman.

35. Sullivan, PL. 2010. "Influenza Vaccination in Health-Care Workers: Should It Be Mandatory?" *Journal of Issues in Nursing.*

36. John Dahlberg-Acton (1834–1902), *Wikipedia.*

12

HPV Vaccinations Should Be Given to All Adolescent Girls

Kristin Klein and Sherry Luedtke

Kristin Klein is a clinical assistant professor of pharmacy at the University of Michigan's College of Pharmacy. Sherry Luedtke is an associate professor of pharmacy practice and a founding faculty member of the School of Pharmacy at Texas Tech University. Klein and Luedtke are members of the Pediatric Pharmacy Advocacy Group.

With an emphasis on religious beliefs, civil rights, and cost concerns, decisions for immunization mandates may not highlight the public health benefits. Recommendations for vaccinating girls and young women against the human papillomavirus (HPV) are no exception. However, HPV is arguably the most common sexually transmitted disease (STD) in the United States, and two strains are associated with almost all cervical cancers. Therefore, all adolescent girls should be given the vaccine before becoming sexually active as well as young women up to twenty-six years of age. Considering the controversy of this recommendation, parents or caregivers should have the authority to vaccinate their children against HPV or not.

Each year, the Centers for Disease Control and Prevention's (CDC) Advisory Committee on Immunization Practices (ACIP) and the American Academy of Pediatrics (AAP) develop and publish their recommended routine pediatric im-

Kristin Klein and Sherry Luedtke, "Human Papillomavirus Vaccination: A Case for Mandatory Immunization?," www.ppag.org, February 15, 2008. Copyright © 2008 by ppag.org. All rights reserved. Reproduced with permission.

munization schedule. The recommendations for immunization practice within this schedule are developed based on the risk/benefit for an individual child as well as the public health benefit. These vaccines, which are recommended but not mandated by the CDC, are generally required for enrollment or admission to state-funded schools and daycare centers. Mandates for immunization are usually determined by the state legislatures. Some states do allow parents to decline vaccinations for medical, religious or "conscientious reasons" which may affect immunization coverage rates and potentially negate the impact and overall benefit to the public.

The decisions to mandate immunizations recommended by the CDC are often influenced by lobbyists who may not focus on the public health benefits of an immunization policy, but rather focus on things such as religious beliefs, individual rights, and financial concerns. Frequently parents are pulled into the controversy and provided misinformation or partial information, which clouds their ability to make individual decisions for their own children. Such is the case with the new human papillomavirus (HPV) immunization recommendations. At present, numerous state legislatures are wrestling with the decision to mandate HPV vaccination of adolescent females. The fact that HPV vaccination provides protection against a sexually transmitted communicable disease adds another level of controversy. This statement attempts to clarify the controversy to assist parents/guardians in making informed decisions regarding the immunization of their children.

Epidemiology

Human papillomavirus (HPV) is likely the most common sexually transmitted disease in the United States, with more than 6 million people becoming infected each year. Of those who become newly infected, 74% are between the ages of 15 and 24 years. Persistent infection with HPV is a known risk factor for the development of cervical cancer. In 2003, 100%

of the cervical cancers reported to the CDC were positive for a cancer-causing type of HPV, 70% of which were due to HPV types 16 or 18. The CDC estimates that approximately 11,000 women will be diagnosed with cervical cancer this year [2008] alone in the United States, with more than 3,500 women dying as a result of cervical cancer. Estimates of HPV infection demonstrate that >80% of sexually active women will become infected with HPV by the time they reach the age of 50 years. Although not as commonly isolated, men are also frequently infected with HPV.

Two strains of HPV, HPV 16 & 18, have been associated with 70–80% of "high grade" or precancerous cervical lesions.

The ACIP currently recommends that the HPV vaccine be administered to adolescent girls during their 11–12 year check-up, prior to when most adolescent girls reach their "sexual debut." A survey conducted annually by the CDC evaluating high-risk behaviors in adolescents revealed that in 2005, 62.4% of girls and 63.8% of boys were sexually active by the time they entered 12th grade. Additionally, 3.7% of adolescent girls and 8.8% of adolescent boys reported becoming sexually active before the age of 13. In 2005, 12% of adolescent girls and 16.5% of adolescent boys reported having 4 or more sexual partners, which is another major risk factor for contracting HPV infection.

Each year, approximately $4 billion is spent on HPV management. The majority of these health-care dollars are spent on follow-up for abnormal Pap smears and on treatment for cervical cancer. Besides the economic burden of HPV infection, a significant emotional burden may occur in a woman with an abnormal Pap smear or who requires a hysterectomy for treatment of cervical cancer.

Pathophysiology

The human papilloma virus (HPV) commonly infects the genital tract, but may also infect the respiratory tract of infants born to an infected mother. It is primarily transmitted via sexual contact, but has been shown to transmit through direct skin contact of lesions. This virus replicates in the squamous epithelial cells and has been associated with cervical cancer as well as other anogenital cancers, anogenital warts, and recurrent respiratory papillomatosis. Over 100 strains of HPV have been identified, however only 40 have been shown to infect the genital tract. Although an acute infection may be clinically evident by the presence of genital lesions or warts, the majority of infected individuals are unaware of their infection and may, thus, transmit it to others. Infections with HPV typically resolve without clinical complications within 1 year. Approximately 10–15% of infections remain persistent which poses a risk of invasive cervical carcinoma and other anogential carcinomas.

Vaccination in early adolescence is recommended to obtain an adequate immune response prior to the sexual debut.

Although relatively few HPV infections lead to cervical cancer, almost all (99%) cervical cancer in women is associated with a previous HPV infection. Two strains of HPV, HPV 16 & 18, have been associated with 70–80% of "high grade" or precancerous cervical lesions. These strains are the primary target for the prevention of cervical cancer in the currently marketed HPV vaccine as well as additional vaccines currently under investigation. In addition, HPV strains 6 & 11 have been associated with > 90% of all genital warts and approximately 10% of "low grade" or low risk cervical lesions, thus vaccination against these strains provides additional benefit.

Individuals infected with one strain of HPV are not protected from infections against other strains, thus repeated infections can occur through one's lifetime.

Immunization

Currently only one HPV vaccine, Gardasil (Merck), is commercially available, however other HPV vaccines are under development. This vaccine is composed of virus like particles (VLPs) or proteins from strains 6, 11, 16 and 18 which self-assemble into structures that immunologically resemble surface structures of HPV. The current vaccine, Gardasil, is formulated with an aluminum adjuvant to enhance the immune response to the protein components. Gardasil is frequently referred to as a quadrivalent vaccine since it is composed of VLPs from the 4 strains that commonly cause infections, HPV 6, 11, 16 & 18. Gardasil is approved by the FDA [US Food and Drug Administration] for females 9–26 years of age for prevention of cervical cancer, genital warts and some precancerous lesions caused by HPV types 6, 11, 16 or 18. Cervarix (GlaxoSmithKline), an HPV vaccine which is awaiting FDA approval, only covers HPV strains 16 & 18. [It was approved in October 2009.]

As previously mentioned, routine vaccination with the HPV vaccine is recommended for females at 11–12 years of age, although the vaccine may be administered from 9 to 26 years of age. Vaccination involves a 3 dose series administered at baseline, 2, and 6 months. Antibody responses to vaccination have been shown to be higher than that observed from natural infection. Vaccination has been shown to be 90% effective in reducing persistent HPV infections and the risk for cervical dysplasia and 99% effective in preventing disease such as genital warts or lesions.

Vaccination in early adolescence is recommended to obtain an adequate immune response prior to the sexual debut. Long term immunogenicity following HPV vaccination is unknown with follow-up studies of antibody responses documented out only to 5 years; antibody levels decline during the first 18 months after vaccination then stabilize at 3.5 years after vaccination. This is similar to what was observed with the Hepatitis B vaccination, for which we know that waning antibody levels are not associated with waning immunity. Postmarketing surveillance will determine the need for future booster vaccination.

Patients who have been previously infected with at least one type of HPV in the vaccine should still be vaccinated since the vaccine will be effective in preventing infection from the 3 other serotypes in the vaccine. The role of HPV vaccination in males is currently under investigation, although studies have shown similar antibody responses as have been observed in females. The societal benefits of male vaccination for the prevention of female infections is yet to be delineated, although some indicate this may not be cost-effective.

Controversy

Vaccination against HPV is a controversial topic for many reasons, including: (1) safety of vaccines, in general; (2) moral objections; (3) perceived risk of increased promiscuity in adolescents; (4) long term efficacy of the vaccine; (5) vaccine availability; (6) cost; and (7) gender discrimination.

Following the very real association between the old rotavirus vaccine (Rotashield®) and intussusception [serious intestinal disorder] and the unsubstantiated link between the measles, mumps and rubella (MMR) vaccine and autism, the public is much less confident in the safety of vaccines than they used to be. Although we can never be entirely sure that a new vaccine or drug will be completely safe in every person who receives it, safety studies of the quadrivalent HPV vaccine (Gardasil®) have not revealed significant adverse effects. The most common adverse effects reported are injection site related (e.g. pain, redness, swelling).

Since the HPV vaccine protects against a sexually transmitted disease (STD), considerable debate regarding the vaccine revolves around the moral implications. People who object to the HPV vaccine on moral grounds usually do so for one of two reasons: (1) for fear that providing a vaccine against an STD will increase sexual activity among adolescents and (2) vaccination is unnecessary since premarital sex is immoral and adolescents should abstain from having sex. Several studies have shown adolescents' sexual activity is not influenced by the availability of condoms or emergency contraception, but has more to do with religious objections and fear of pregnancy. It is important, however, to keep in mind that 6.2% of all adolescents are sexually active by the age of 13 years and 63.1% are sexually active by the time they enter 12th grade. Parents need to be cognizant of this fact when making the decision of whether to vaccinate their children.

As further information becomes available regarding factors such as feasibility of mandatory vaccination and the role of vaccinating males in decreasing HPV transmission, decisions regarding HPV vaccination may become less controversial.

From a cost standpoint, the HPV vaccine is fairly costly at $120 per dose ($360 for the 3-dose series). Since the vaccine has been added to the recommended childhood immunization schedule, the Vaccines for Children program should cover the cost of the vaccine in eligible adolescents. Many insurers are covering the cost of vaccination for females, but not males since the vaccine is not approved for use in males.

For practitioners, some additional questions regarding the HPV vaccine still need to be addressed, including those regarding vaccine availability. Now that the vaccine has been added to the childhood immunization schedule, will vaccine supply be able to keep up with demand? This has been an issue with some vaccines recently, including the Tdap (tetanus, diphtheria and reduced acellular pertussis) and meningococcal conjugate vaccines. The feasibility of achieving complete immunization with the 3-dose series in the adolescent population, which historically is frequently lost to medical follow-up, remains a concern. The long-term efficacy of the quadrivalent vaccine remains unknown. To date, efficacy studies have only followed vaccine recipients for a maximum of 5 years. In the future, will booster doses be required?

Recommendations

The Pediatric Pharmacy Advocacy Group (PPAG) endorses the safety and efficacy of the quadrivalent HPV vaccine and agrees that the vaccine should be recommended for all adolescent girls, preferably prior to their "sexual debut." Furthermore, we agree that the HPV vaccine should be recommended to young women through the age of 26 years to decrease the risk of contracting a cancer-causing strain of HPV, even if they are already sexually active. PPAG acknowledges that the decision to vaccinate an adolescent against HPV is controversial and believes that parents and/or caregivers should be able to choose whether or not to vaccinate their adolescents. As further information becomes available regarding factors such as feasibility of mandatory vaccination and the role of vaccinating males in decreasing HPV transmission, decisions regarding HPV vaccination may become less controversial.

13

HPV Vaccinations Should Not Be Mandatory

Susan M. Haack

Based in Mauston, Wisconsin, Susan M. Haack is a gynecologist and associate fellow with The Center for Bioethics & Human Dignity.

Mandatory human papillomavirus (HPV) vaccinations for adolescent girls may create more problems than they prevent. While the virus is widespread, genital warts and cervical cancer affect small percentages of the population. Vaccination is also recommended at the age of eleven or twelve, before the onset of sexual activity. But HPV is largely transient in this group, and the vaccine may not offer protection in adulthood, when immunity weakens and cervical cancer appears. Finally, mandatory HPV vaccinations would financially strain the health-care system and violate adolescents' right to informed consent. The aggressive promotion of the vaccine signifies the shift in American medicine from preventing diseases to accommodating risky lifestyle choices.

The United States has the most affluent and technologically advanced healthcare system in the developed world, offering increased life-expectancy and quality of life to many. Yet it is also the most inequitable system in the developed world, with many of its own residents lacking access to this system of

Susan M. Haack, "HPV Vaccine: Panacea or Pandora's Box? The Costs and Deceptiveness of the New Technology," cbhd.org, February 4, 2011. http://cbhd.org/content/hpv-vaccine-panacea-or-pandora's-box-costs-and-deceptiveness-new-technology. The text included below is an excerpted version, and the original with full citations is available at www.cbhd.org, the website for The Center for Bioethics & Human Dignity. Reproduced with permission.

care—a fact which weighs heavily on our national conscience. Consequently, healthcare reform is again an urgent political issue, with the most recent reform package estimated to cost over $3 trillion to institute.

It is in this context that one of the newer technological advances, HPV (human papilloma virus) vaccination, must be evaluated. The first quadrivalent vaccine was licensed for use in 2006 but not widely utilized until the completion of phase three trials in 2007. Even though the clinically relevant end-point of this trial was the prevention of CIN (cervical intraepithelial neoplasia) II and III, it was quickly marketed as the first cancer vaccine: if administered to preadolescent girls, before the onset of sexual activity, it would prevent the later development of cervical cancer. This was rapidly followed by an egregiously premature move to make vaccination against HPV a mandatory requirement through the school system, a move which lacked the empirical foundation necessary to withstand critical opposition, except in the state of Texas.

What Is HPV?

Human papilloma virus is a DNA virus that is transmitted by skin-to-skin contact, and is similar to papilloma viruses that cause "warts" on other areas of the body. There are approximately 40 species that specifically infect the genital tract, causing genital warts and—in the presence of other co-factors, such as smoking or immune deficiency—cancers of the cervix, vagina, and vulva. While the virus is more prevalent in men, they rarely develop significant consequences of infection. The virus has been isolated on sperm, but skin-to-skin contact is the primary means of transmission with scrotal skin serving as a passive reservoir for male-female transmission. It is the incorporation of viral DNA into the genome of the infected cell that produces cellular changes leading to clinical "disease."

Historical Perspective

Our understanding of the mechanism of infection with HPV has changed significantly over the past 30 years, from permanence to transience; from general to specific; and from progression to regression. Originally, infection was felt to be a permanent condition, much like that seen with herpes viruses. Conversely, in recent years we have come to understand that infections with HPV are most often transient, with the median duration of infection ranging from 4.8 months for low risk viruses to 8.1 months for high risk viruses, and with clearance rates as high as 92% in 2–5 years.

Since the duration of protection is unknown and the average age of diagnosis of cervical cancer is 45, it has not been demonstrated that the vaccination of all 11–12 year olds will prevent cancer at age 45.

Moreover, the infection is most transient in young girls, with women over 30 less able and less likely to clear the virus. Secondly, whereas all species of HPV were originally thought to carry a risk of cervical cancer, we now know that these genital viruses have differing oncogenic potential; they are therefore categorized as either "low risk" or "high risk" based on the potential to initiate malignant and premalignant changes in the cervical epithelium. It is the oncogenic ("high risk") viruses that raise serious medical concern. The third significant change in our understanding is that just as the infection is not permanent, neither is the disease necessarily progressive: mild precancerous changes do not necessarily and inexorably lead to cancer, as we once believed. Most often the changes are regressive: with clearance of the virus, the virally-induced cellular changes also regress. Therefore, attempting to eradicate all virally-induced changes is no longer believed to be necessary nor is it recommended.

The Burden of HPV

The prevalence of HPV has increased exponentially in recent years concurrent with the exponential increase in promiscuous sexual activity in our culture. There are currently 24 million people in the U.S. infected with the virus, including 26–35% of sexually active couples. Moreover, there is an 80% chance of acquiring the virus by age 50. Generally speaking, subclinical infection, in which the virus is present but virally-induced cellular changes are absent, is 10–30 times more common than clinical infection, but often clears spontaneously. Clinical infections include genital warts (~1% of the population), laryngeal papillomatosis, cervical dysplasia, and cervical, vulvar, and vaginal cancers. Cervical cancer is diagnosed in 11,000 women each year with 3,500 women dying yearly from the disease. The average age at diagnosis is 45.

The monetary burden of this virus is not insignificant. The cost of screening, testing, and treating HPV in the year 2000 was $3 billion ($3.4 billion if costs of treating cancer were included). In that same year, $167 million was spent to treat genital warts.

Concerns with Vaccination

HPV vaccines have proven to be 100% effective in preventing the neoplastic changes associated with HPV 16 and 18, and 100% effective in preventing genital warts resulting from infection with HPV 6 and 11. Yet in spite of these positive statistics, there are significant concerns. In order to be effective, a vaccine must be administered before the onset of sexual activity and hence before exposure to the viruses. The ideal age of vaccination has therefore been determined to be 11–12. But the virus is highly transient in adolescents in whom cervical cancer has never been diagnosed, and the duration of protection from the vaccination is unknown. It is therefore possible that the protective effects of the vaccination will wane at the time when women are most susceptible to the oncogenic effects of the virus (those over 30), providing protection to those who do not need it (adolescents) and failing to provide protection to those who do (women over 30).

Secondly, the quadrivalent vaccine covers only 4 of the approximately 40 papilloma viruses that infect the genital tract (HPV 6, 11, 16 and 18). The newer bivalent vaccine released this past year covers only HPV 16 and 18. HPV 6 and 11 are low risk viruses that will resolve spontaneously within one year, rendering any vaccine against them a waste of valuable resources and healthcare dollars. HPV 16 and 18 have oncogenic potential, but even 80% of these infections will resolve without treatment. Additionally, the four HPV types covered by the vaccine account for only 3.4% of all HPV infections in the U.S., and HPV 16 and 18 account for only 2.3% of the high risk viral infections in the U.S. (HPV 6: 1.3%; HPV 11: 0.1%; HPV 16: 1.5%; and HPV 18: 0.8%). Moreover, not all of those who acquire these two viruses will develop cervical cancer. Even the American College of Obstetricians and Gynecologists states that "very few individuals with an HPV infection will develop cancer." Since the duration of protection is unknown and the average age of diagnosis of cervical cancer is 45, it has not been demonstrated that the vaccination of all 11–12 year olds will prevent cancer at age 45. There is no long term data to support such a program, only speculation based on "knowledge" that is incomplete and ever-evolving.

What is the ethically appropriate response when disagreement exists between the mother and the daughter with regard to the vaccination or completion of the series?

Under naturally occurring circumstances, infection with HPV triggers an immune response that provides a natural source of protection against the virus. Vaccination may inhibit this response, and if the vaccination then fails to provide permanent protection, these once-vaccinated young women will also lack any natural immunity, rendering them more susceptible to infection at a time when they are also more vulnerable to the oncogenic potential of the virus. Additionally, there is some concern that vaccination may generate shifts in oncogenic potential, escalating the risk of other viral strains for which there is no vaccine, a phenomenon recognized with influenza viruses.

Concerns with Cost Effectiveness

HPV vaccines are exorbitantly expensive, exceeding the cost of all other vaccinations combined, and making it unfeasible for use in the general population. At a cost of $500–900 for the series of 3 injections, vaccination will be inaccessible to many, thereby diminishing the overall effectiveness through loss of "herd immunity." And in spite of its price-tag, it does not eliminate costs of screening that are currently utilized: due to the large number of other viruses not covered by the vaccine, current screening methods will still be required.

The cost-effectiveness of vaccination is dependent upon a reduction in the rate of cervical cancer, an effect that has not to date been proven, which will not be realized for 4 or 5 decades, and which is dependent on achieving a high level of protection among a substantial portion of the population. And at a time when cost of medical care is under scrutiny, the crucial question is: who will pay? A recent study determined that if the protection the vaccination offered was permanent, vaccination of 11–12 year olds would cost an additional $43,600 per QALY [quality-adjusted life year], over and above the cost of current screening methods, a level that was felt to fall within the range of cost-effectiveness. However, if a booster is required, the cost-effectiveness of the vaccination will be further diminished. And logic belies the data: to vaccinate 10 million 11–12 year olds each year will cost approximately $5 billion/year, a cost which will merely diminish the risk of cervical cancer from HPV 16/18 for approximately 4,600 women.

And these women will still be at risk for cervical cancer from other or new oncogenic strains of virus, as it is estimated that 50% of vaccinated women will still develop high grade cervical lesions due to the other viruses. The high prevalence of these viruses, the transience of infection, the low prevalence of the virus in question, and the low incidence of serious disease would argue against cost-effectiveness of the vaccine and suggest that despite the rigorous statistical analysis employed by this study, a methodological error exists.

Concerns with Informed Consent

One of the cornerstones of modern medical practice is that of informed consent. The risks, benefits, side effects and alternatives of any medical procedure must be discussed with the patient before it is performed. Where a procedure is felt to be "necessary," however, informed consent is often glossed over, if not ignored. And so it is with this vaccine, especially given the speed with which it received FDA [US Food and Drug Administration] approval. But the vaccination is not without associated risks—risks which potentially exceed the theoretical benefit—and these include paralysis, blood clots, Guillain-Barré syndrome, and death. There have been 43 reports of deaths (26 confirmed, 9 under investigation, and 8 unconfirmed) among young women associated with the vaccine, yet death from cervical cancer is unknown in adolescents. At age 11 or 12, informed consent is often given to and by the parent or guardian. Is the adolescent being informed? Is she being educated? While mandates and coercion might be warranted in epidemics where public health and safety are at risk, this is not the case with HPV infection. And what is the ethically appropriate response when disagreement exists between the mother and the daughter with regard to the vaccination or completion of the series? The HPV vaccine has been marketed as a vaccination against cervical cancer, yet there is no data to substantiate that the vaccine prevents cervical cancer or that vaccinating adolescents today will indeed prevent cervical cancer later. Such marketing is deceptive and manipulative. Is this being addressed in our "informed consent"? Furthermore, the marketing techniques deceptively promote a false sense of security by placing emphasis on the rare oncogenic consequences of infection rather than on the nature of the virus as an STD. In so doing, it fails to acknowledge that the most cost-effective means of preventing cervical cancer is not a vaccine but cessation of smoking (a known co-factor for cervical cancer) and abstinence until marriage for both males and females. It is unlikely that this is part of the informed consent process even though it is one of the alternatives that comprise informed consent and an educational responsibility of healthcare providers.

The burden of this vaccine as well as the infection falls again to the female population. The vaccine has not been tested on males and perhaps for good economic reason: males serve primarily as vectors for the virus, in most cases suffering no significant short- or long-term consequences from infection. It would be a rare young man—or mother of a young man—who would subject himself to the cost, the pain, and the inconvenience of the vaccine for the sake of women 40 years hence.

From a global perspective, HPV vaccination may indeed be a panacea by providing protection where screening is unavailable. But third world countries do not have the resources from which companies can recover their expenses. Conversely, while we in the U.S. have the fiscal resources, we also have a screening program that has proven to be cost-effective in preventing cervical cancer, if utilized. Pap smear screening is also more cost-effective than vaccination, since it is nondiscriminatory with respect to viral types.

A Shift in American Medicine

There has been a subtle but significant paradigm shift in the orientation of American medicine in recent years from preventing and treating illnesses to alleviating the consequences of life-style choices. That shift is costing us greatly, as our choices are boundless and our perceived need insatiable. The rapid, deceptive, and pervasive promotion of the HPV vaccine is illustrative of this shift and raises more questions than answers. Experience in other areas of medicine (osteoporosis, coronary artery disease) has demonstrated that positive changes in clinical markers do not always correlate with disease prevention. With the rapid evolution in our understanding of HPV, it is imprudent to base disease prevention on clinical information that is incomplete and unproven. Given what we do know, the vaccine makes little sense. Why are we vaccinating young women with an expensive, painful vaccine that has not been proven to prevent what it claims? Why are we advocating that all pre-adolescent young women be vaccinated against an uncommon virus that is known to be largely transient? It calls into question the methodological assumptions underlying the research for the vaccine. The original research was initiated in 1991. Was this under the earlier assumption that the viral infection was permanent, before the transient nature of the infection was known? Now that the vaccine has been developed, does it have to be marketed in order to recover the expenses of the research and development? Why has it been marketed when the long-term effects on the immune system of young girls and the oncogenic potential of other viruses are unknown?

Are we perhaps creating more problems than we are preventing? And finally, is this an effective use of scarce medical resources and dollars? These are questions that should have been answered prior to FDA approval, but will need to be answered in the days ahead if we are to preserve a system of healthcare that is accessible to all of our citizens.

Organizations to Contact

The editors have compiled the following list of organizations concerned with the issues debated in this book. The descriptions are derived from materials provided by the organizations. All have publications or information available for interested readers. The list was compiled on the date of publication of the present volume; names, addresses, phone and fax numbers, and e-mail and Internet addresses may change. Be aware that many organizations take several weeks or longer to respond to inquiries, so allow as much time as possible.

Association of American Physicians and Surgeons (AAPS)
1601 N Tucson Blvd., #9, Tucson, AZ 85716
(800) 635-1196 • fax: (520) 325-4230
e-mail: aaps@aapsonline.org
website: www.aapsonline.org

The Association of American Physicians and Surgeons (AAPS) is a national association of physicians dedicated to preserving freedom in the one-on-one patient-physician relationship. AAPS fights in the courts for the rights of patients and physicians, sponsors seminars for physicians, testifies before committees in Congress, and educates the public. Among the news briefs and publications available at the AAPS website are a fact sheet on mandatory vaccines and the organization's resolution concerning mandatory vaccines.

Centers for Disease Control and Prevention (CDC)
1600 Clifton Road, Atlanta, GA 30333
(800) 232-4636
website: www.cdc.gov

The Centers for Disease Control and Prevention (CDC), a part of the US Department of Health and Human Services, is the primary federal agency conducting and supporting public health activities in the United States. Through research and education, the CDC is dedicated to protecting health and promoting quality of life through the prevention and control of disease, injury, and disability. Among the many publications available on the CDC's website regarding vaccines and immunizations are childhood, adolescent, and adult immunization schedules; information about reasons to vaccinate and the importance of vaccinating; and vaccine safety reports, including access to the Vaccine Adverse Event Reporting System (VAERS).

Commonwealth Fund

1 E 75th St., New York, NY   10021
(212) 606-3800 • fax: (212) 606-3500
e-mail: info@cmwf.org
website: www.commonwealthfund.org

The Commonwealth Fund is a private foundation that aims to promote a high-performing healthcare system that achieves better patient access, improved quality, and greater efficiency, particularly for society's most vulnerable populations, including low-income people, the uninsured, minority Americans, young children, and elderly adults. The Commonwealth Fund carries out this mandate by supporting independent research on healthcare issues and making grants to improve healthcare practice and policy. The foundation publishes the *Commonwealth Fund Digest* and offers performance snapshots, including one on the issue of immunizing young children, available on its website.

Immunization Action Coalition (IAC)

1573 Selby Ave., Suite 234, St. Paul, MN   55104
(651) 647-9009 • fax: (651) 647-9131
e-mail: admin@immunize.org
website: www.immunize.org

Immunization Action Coalition (IAC) works to increase immunization rates and prevent disease and creates educational materials and facilitates communication about the safety, efficacy, and use of vaccines within the broad immunization community of patients, parents, healthcare organizations, and government health agencies. The IAC publishes numerous brochures and vaccination schedules, including the brochures, "What If You Don't Immunize Your Child?" and "After the Shots. . ."

Institute for Vaccine Safety (IVS)

Johns Hopkins Bloomberg School of Public Health
615 N. Wolfe St., Room W5041, Baltimore, MD   21205
website: www.vaccinesafety.edu

The Institute for Vaccine Safety (IVS) aims to obtain and disseminate objective information about the safety of recommended immunizations. It provides a forum for dissemination of data regarding specific issues concerning the safety of immunizations, investigates safety questions, and conducts research. IVS also sponsors academic publications about vaccinations and provides information about state school vaccination law exemptions and vaccine legislation.

National Network for Immunization Information (NNii)

301 University Blvd., Galveston, TX   77555-0350
(702) 200-0201 • fax: (409) 772-5208
e-mail: dipineda@utmb.edu
website: www.immunizationinfo.org

The National Network for Immunization Information (NNii) is affiliated with the Infectious Diseases Society of America, Pediatric Infectious Diseases Society, American Academy of Pediatrics, American Nurses Association, and other organizations. The network provides the public, health professionals, policymakers, and the media with up-to-date immunization information to help clarify the issues and help people make informed decisions regarding immunization. NNii publishes numerous briefs, papers, and pamphlets, including "Exemptions from Immunization Laws" and "Evaluating Information About Vaccines on the Internet" available on its website.

National Vaccine Information Center (NVIC)

21525 Ridgetop Circle, Suite 100, Sterling, VA   20166
(703) 938-0342 • fax: (571) 313-1268
e-mail: contactnvic@gmail.com
website: www.nvic.org

The National Vaccine Information Center (NVIC) is dedicated to defending the right to informed consent to medical interventions and to preventing vaccine injuries and deaths through public education. NVIC provides assistance to those who have suffered vaccine reactions; promotes research to evaluate vaccine safety and effectiveness; and monitors vaccine research, development, regulation, policy making and legislation. Many resources are available on the center's website, including position papers and articles and a vaccine ingredients calculator.

ThinkTwice Global Vaccine Institute

PO Box 9638, Santa Fe, NM   87504
e-mail: think@thinktwice.com
website: www.thinktwice.com

The ThinkTwice Global Vaccine Institute was established in 1996 to provide parents and other concerned people with educational resources to help them make more-informed vaccine decisions. ThinkTwice encourages an uncensored exchange of vaccine information and supports every family's right to accept or reject vaccines. The institute offers various studies, articles, and books on its website, including the book *Vaccines: Are They Really Safe and Effective?*

Vaccination Liberation

PO Box 457, Spirit Lake, ID   83869-0457
e-mail: info@vaccinetruth.com
website: www.vaclib.org

Vaccination Liberation is part of a national grassroots network dedicated to providing information, not often made available to the public, about vaccinations, with the goal of encouraging people to avoid and refuse vaccines. Vaccination

Liberation works to dispute claims that vaccines are necessary, safe, and effective; expand awareness of alternatives in health care; preserve the right to abstain from vaccination; and repeal all compulsory vaccination laws nationwide. The organization offers various publications on its website, including the book *The Vaccine Religion: Mass Mind & the Struggle for Human Freedom.*

Vaccine Education Center
The Children's Hospital of Philadelphia
34th St. and Civic Center Blvd., Philadelphia, PA 19104
(215) 590-1000
website: www.chop.edu/service/vaccine-education-center

The Vaccine Education Center at the Children's Hospital of Philadelphia educates parents and healthcare providers about vaccines and immunizations. The center provides videos, informational tear sheets, and other information about every vaccine. Among these numerous publications available for download on the center's website are the booklets *Vaccines and Your Baby* and *Vaccines and Teens.*

Bibliography

Books

Arthur Allen   *Vaccine: The Controversial Story of Medicine's Greatest Lifesaver*. New York: W.W. Norton, 2007.

Andrew W. Artenstein, ed.   *Vaccines: A Biography*. New York: Springer, 2010.

William R. Clark   *In Defense of Self: How the Immune System Really Works*. New York: Oxford University Press, 2008.

Robert Goldberg   *Tabloid Medicine: How the Internet Is Being Used to Hijack Medical Science for Fear and Profit*. New York: Kaplan, 2010.

Richard Halvorsen   *The Truth About Vaccines: Making the Right Decision for Your Child*, 2nd ed. London, United Kingdom: Gibson Square, 2009.

Stacy Mintzer Herlihy and E. Allison Hagood   *Your Baby's Best Shot: Why Vaccines Are Safe and Save Lives*. Lanham, MD: Rowman & Littlefield Publishers, 2012.

Kendall Hoyt   *Long Shot: Vaccines for National Defense*. Cambridge, MA: Harvard University Press, 2011.

Mark A. Largent   *Vaccine: The Debate in Modern America*. Baltimore, MD: Johns Hopkins University Press, 2012.

Deborah Mitchell *The Essential Guide to Children's Vaccines.* New York: St. Martin's Press, 2012.

Seth Mnookin *The Panic Virus: A True Story of Medicine, Science, and Fear.* New York: Simon & Schuster, 2011.

Andreas Moritz *Vaccine-Nation: Poisoning the Population, One Shot at a Time.* Brevard, NC: Ener-Chi Wellness Press, 2011.

Paul A. Offit *Deadly Choices: How the Anti-Vaccine Movement Threatens Us All.* New York: Basic Books, 2011.

Paul A. Offit and Charlotte A. Moser *Vaccines & Your Child: Separating Fact from Fiction.* New York: Columbia University Press, 2011.

Manmohan Singh and Indresh K. Srivastava, eds. *Development of Vaccines: From Discovery to Clinical Testing.* Hoboken, NJ: John Wiley & Sons, 2011.

Andrew J. Wakefield *Callous Disregard: Autism and Vaccines—The Truth Behind a Tragedy.* New York: Skyhorse Publishing, 2010.

Periodicals and Internet Sources

Christina England "The Most Dangerous Greeting Your Child May Ever Receive," Vactruth.com, April 15, 2013.

Nan Feyler — "In the Fight Against Cancer, a Vaccine Is Underused," The Public's Health, October 10, 2012. www .philly.com.

Miriam Fine-Goulden — "Should Childhood Vaccination Be Compulsory in the UK?," *Opticon1826*, Spring 2010. www .opticon1826.com.

Daniel Goodman and Christopher Webster — "The Mandatory Vaccination of Health Care Workers," *Law Practice Today*, April 2011.

Matthew Helper — "The Gardasil Problem: How the US Lost Faith in a Promising Vaccine," *Forbes*, April 23, 2012.

Xian Wen Jin, Andrea Sikon, and Ellen Rome — "Human Papillomavirus Vaccine: Safe, Effective, Underused," *Cleveland Clinic Journal of Medicine*, January 2013.

Fran Lowry — "Mandatory Vaccination of Healthcare Workers a Success," Medscape, June 17, 2013. www .medscape.com.

Amanda Mascarelli — "Doctors See Chinks in Vaccination Armor," *Los Angeles Times*, August 5, 2011.

Michelle M. Mello, Sara Abiola, and James Colgrove — "Pharmaceutical Companies' Role in State Vaccination Policymaking: The Case of Human Papillomavirus Vaccination," *American Journal of Public Health*, May 2012.

Alex Newman   "Swine Flu: The Risks and Efficacy of
                     Vaccines," *New American*, October 14,
                     2009. www.thenewamerican.com.

Alan Phillips   "Vaccine Exemptions: Do They Really
                     Put Others at Risk?," *Natural News*,
                     February 18, 2012. www.naturalnews
                     .com.

Olav Phillips   "Everything You Always Wanted to
                     Know About Cancer, Sex, and the
                     Mandatory Human Papilloma
                     Vaccine," *Paranoia Magazine*,
                     November 6, 2012. www
                     .paranoiamagazine.com.

David M.   "Should Vaccines Be Mandatory?
Salisbury   No," *British Medical Journal*, May 15,
                     2012.

Margaret Wente   "Autism, Vaccines, and Fear," *Globe &
                     Mail*, February 4, 2010.

Cheryl Wetzstein   "Doctors Call for HPV Shots for
                     Boys," *Washington Times*, February
                     27, 2012. www.washingtontimes.com.

Index